To Miriam & Chaim
in treasured friendship –

[illegible]

Murray [illegible]

July 9, 79

[illegible]

The voice of my blood cries out

The voice of my blood cries out

The Holocaust as reflected in Hebrew poetry

by

Murray J. Kohn

Shengold Publishers, Inc.
New York City

ISBN 0-88400-063-X

Library of Congress Catalog Card Number: 78-66108

Published by Shengold Publishers, Inc.
New York, N.Y.

Printed in the United States of America

This book is dedicated to the memory of the Six Million of my brethren, two of whom were my beloved mother and sister, and to my beloved father who risked his life in Auschwitz to sustain me.

CONTENTS

PREFACE

There is no author who is not indebted to a number of individuals whose guidance, encouragement and support have been invaluable to him. This study is no exception.

Primarily, I am indebted to my teacher and mentor, Professor Judah Pilch, who has guided and inspired me from the very inception of my doctoral dissertation, originally written in Hebrew, to its present enlarged English edition.

The encouragement I received from Elie Wiesel, the most eloquent spokesman and author of the Holocaust era, after he read the Hebrew manuscript, had a great impact on me.

Thanks, too, are due to the poets Aharon Zeitlin z"l, Yehudah Leib Bialer z"l, Israel Efros, Shimon Halkin and Chaim Chamiel whom I personally interviewed and whose advice and observations were invaluable to my research.

No less do I value the assistance and expertise of Dr. Joseph Kermish, Director of the Holocaust Archieves, Dr. H. Rosenkrantz, and Mr. M. Piekarz, the brilliant bibliographer, all of Yad Vashem in Jerusalem.

My thanks go the the wonderful librarians and reference assitants of The National Library at the Hebrew University in Jerusalem, the Zionist Archives of Jerusalem, the Zionist Archives in New York City, Yivo Library in New York City, Dropsie University Library in Philadephia, Jewish Theological Seminary in New York City, the New York City Public Library Jewish Division at 42nd Street and, particularly, the Library of the New York Hebrew Union College-Jewish Institute of Religion with its extensive collections of Modern Hebrew Literature.

A special thanks goes to the erudite Dr. Ida Cohen Selavan of Pittsburgh, Pa., who has with great care and skill read and edited the manuscript.

Above all, I wish to express my gratitude to my beloved wife, Beverly, and our wonderful daughters, Martha and Sara, whose love and patience made it possible to complete this study.

I cherish also the support, encouragement and generosity I received from so many of my friends and congregants of Beth Israel Congregation of Vineland, N.J. I shall always remember the warm and affectionate tribute they paid me in December of 1978.

To my publisher, Mr. Moshe A. Sheinbaum, a special "Thank you" for the "mentschlichkeit" and sensitivity he has shown.

Last but not least, my thanks to Miss Janet Arrigo for preparing the manuscript for the publisher with meticulous care and to my assistant Rabbi Samuel Nunberg for his insightful reading of the manuscript and Mr. Paul Stern M.F.A., for his literary suggestions.

The well known adage *Traduttori Traditori* (Translators-Traitors) will hopefully not be applied too freely in this case since I am both the author and translator of the Hebrew book. I have taken the liberty of expanding some areas and curtailing others in the English version. Thus, responsibility is all mine.

And finally, this study does not pretend to have embraced the totality of Hebrew poetry on the subject of the Holocaust. There are many more themes to be dealt with and still more poetic materials await translation into English.

In several cases I could not help but include a few Yiddish poems in their Hebrew translation in order to complete the thematic illustrations. A number of poems were translated from Moshe Prager's Anthology: *Min Hametzar Karati* which had been translated into Hebrew from the various languages in which they were originally written. Were is not for their translation into Hebrew, they would have remained in the archives. Their translation into Hebrew redeemed them from oblivion. Of central importance is Yitzchak Katzenelson's epic, *"The Song of the Slaughtered Jewish People."* It has become an integral part of Hebrew Poetry even though it was originally written in Yiddish, the predominant langauge of the martyred Jews.

In conclusion, the Holocaust themes were my object and Hebrew poetry my handmaiden, through which to illuminate areas of the Holocaust tragedy which have not heretofore received full consideration.

I hope that this study will serve as a key to unlock great treasures of heretofore hidden sources from the Holocaust era.

If this proves to be the case, my efforts will not have been in vain.

M.J.K.

Vineland, New Jersey

Kislev, 5739 — November, 1978
36th Anniversary of my imprisonment
at Auschwitz.

I

PROLEGOMENON

From its earliest literary history, Hebrew poetry has fulfilled its historical task in reflecting the suffering and anguish of the Jewish people's perennial struggle for survival. In more than one way, it served faithfully as a trusted chronicle of Israel's story.

Thus, the acrostic elegy on the destruction of the First Temple, "The Book of Lamentations," by the traditionally assumed authorship of the prophet Jeremiah, served as a firsthand account of the tragic event.[1] So did the litanies over the persecutions and destructions of Jewish communities in the middle ages.[2] The same is true of Chaim Nachman Bialik's elegy "On The Slaughter"[3] in memory of the 1903 Kishinev pogroms. But none can compare to the soul-shattering, eulogy-like epic by Yitzchak Katzenelson: "The Song of the Slaughtered Jewish People"[4] which he completed shortly before he was taken to his death in the Vitell concentration camp. No less imposing in depth, breadth and scope is Meir Bossak's great dirge: "Mima'amakim" (From The Depths)[5] or the threnodies of Uri Tzvi Greenberg, "Rechovot Hanahar" (The Streets of the River).

These poets reacted to the suffering of our people as a whole and reflected the torment of the individual in particular in his desperation in the throes of annihilation. Thus, poetic verse accompanied those who were marched to the ravines, gallows, gas chambers, and the crematoria, as well as those who participated in the battles of the underground, with the partisans, and in the open battlefield. In short, the strings of the poet's lyre responded to the call of the hour, be it in self-chastisement or lamentation, remorse or despair, outcry or shock, challenging God or resenting one's own fate, and accused a silent world of outright perfidy. No less did it entertain glimmers of hope, reaching the imponderable heights of faith in spite of the impossible predicament. It no less inspired the survivors of the hellish fires to begin anew . . .

Hence, this particular poetry constitutes an incalculably important and lasting contributon to the literature of the Holocaust era. In fact, more than other victims and martyrs of our long history, the Holocaust victims had a profound awareness of history which produced an insatiable desire to immortalize the tragic events in all their horrifying details.

This attitude was succinctly expressed by Yasha Rabinovitz:

> If I was doomed to die for God's sake,
> In behalf of my tortured brethren I make
> A pledge to leave my will in poems.

— *Min Hametzar Karati*

The poet Meir Mohar, who was outside the Holocaust's reach reacted thus:

> And I shall not refrain from a harvest
> of new verses,
> In spite of an anguished soul
> foresaken by God and men.

— *Sod Siach Behalah*

Nevertheless, some reacted with biting criticism or perhaps cynicism against the outpouring of this mass of poetry on the Holocaust theme. It is often difficult to determine against whom this reaction was directed. Thus, for example, A. Domnitz wrote:

> In every inn and in every language, every
> cripple and every stutterer, comes with
> his hoarse Kaddish upon the graves . . .

— *V'acharey He'ason*

And still more scathingly does Shimon ben Eliezer react:

> Enough you shedders of tears!
> Your lyric grates upon our ears.
> Who can tolerate forever the sound

Of your lament over my misfortunes?
Why do you profusely wail and cry
Adding eulogies upon our sorrow
While comfortably ensconsed in an armchair?

— *K'neged Hamekonenim*

Elie Wiesel has offered an instructive and pointed answer to those who criticize the profusion of writings on the Holocaust regardless of their quality or literary genre:

> On his way to the mass grave the historian Simon Dubov exhorts the Jews of Riga, his companions in misfortune: Open your eyes and ears, remember every detail, every name and every whisper, the colors of the clouds, the hissing of the wind in the trees, the executioner's every gesture; the one who survives must forget nothing. Everywhere at the very moment of torture and death, young militants and wizened old men make notes, consign to paper events, anecdotes, impressions. Some are only children: David Rubinstein and Anne Frank. Behind the walls of the Warsaw Ghetto, Emanuel Ringelblum and his hundred scribes have a single thought; to gather and bury as many documents as possible. So much suffering, so many trials must not be lost to history. Since European Jewry is doomed, it becomes imperative to preserve at least the scorched vestiges of its sojourn. Poems, litanies, plays. To write them, writers went without sleep, bartered their food for pencils and paper. They gambled with their fate. They risked their lives. Nothing else mattered. They went on fitting together words and symbols. An instant before perishing, in Auschwitz, in Bialystok, in Buna, dying men described their agony. I attended in Buchenwald several "literary evenings" and listened to anonymous poets reciting verses. I was too young to understand. They did not write for me but for the others. Those outside the camp and those yet unborn. There was then a veritable passion to testify for the future against death and oblivion, a passion conveyed by every possible means of expression.

— *Twenty-Five Years After*

The gifted poets Aharon Zeitlin and Yehuda Leib Bialer (of Blessed Memory), Chaim Chamiel, Simon Halkin, and Israel Efros, have graciously helped me to identify the rudimentary issues which our poetry has attempted to confront which will continue to serve as essential themes for many years to come. It is a matter of coming to grips with the near extermination of one third of the Jewish people in full view of an indifferent world. It is also a matter of our own national conscience, guilt-ridden for having failed to sense the coming onslaught which left European Jewry helpless in its agony and world Jewry unprepared to meet the tragic challenge.

Thus, ever since the tragedy began, our mind has been saturated with rebellion and bitterness; guilt, lament and despair; innocent faith and alienation. The very spiritual foundations of our people have been undermined. A spiritual crisis and a resultant revolution in thought have touched us to the core of our human and Jewish being. Hebrew poetry's sensitivity to these gnawing issues succeeded in touching the soul of our people by focusing upon the existent spiritual crisis and upon other painful issues which deny our people any complacency since the catastrophe.

This is a first attempt to subject the Holocaust and post-Holocaust poetry to a thematic analysis in full view of the major topical aspects of this era. For instance, this study has chosen to examine the reactions of Hebrew poetry to the following topics:

1. Shock, in view of the initial Nazi atrocities;
2. Despair, in view of the growing awareness and realization that all is lost;
3. Accusation and condemnation of the world in view of its silence and utter indifference to the annihilation of the Jewish people;
4. Challenging God for His silence and His supposed abandonment of His people in view of the total destruction of the Jewish masses in Europe. Within the ramifications of this latter topic, the entire gamut of theological speculation is brought into focus, e.g., the questions of Deus Obsconditus; Reward and Punishment; Limitatio Dei; Theodicy; Agonisticism; Fate, Faith and Historic Destiny.
5. Personal confession and collective guilt-feeling, particularly by those who were outside the realm of the Holocaust. This embraces: empathy, anxiety, mental anguish, guilt-feeling and helplessness as much as self-accusation for inaction.

The reason that poetry, in particular, has been chosen for such an analysis, is because it was deemed that poetry, in whichever form or degree, has been the most authentic expression of the immediate personal reaction to the tragedy of the Holocaust. We have also found that in many instances a large segment of personal reaction to the tragedy from the victims themselves, has been written in verse.

In addition, poetry was chosen for reasons of its ability to transform, somehow, the emotions of the moment into words. The tragic events of the Holocaust have been best transmitted in their emotional tenor. The irrationality of the Holocaust, could not lend itself other than to emotional reactions whether it be in documenting an event, reflecting upon the doleful state of the people or persons, or bequeathing one's own testament for the survivors.

This study also attempts to draw a clear distinction between the poetry written by the victims and survivors vis-a-vis the reactions in verse to the Holocaust of those outside the Holocaust area. The distinction becomes quite clear in comparing these parallel creations as to tone, expression, and, oft times, purpose. For example, the victims' main purpose was to leave an authentic expression of themselves for those who would survive the unbelievable tragedy. Only with exception, it should be noted, has this poetry been produced by any professional poets.

On the other hand, the predominant poetry written outside the Nazi area comes from professional poets, whose poetry served as personal expression regarding the tragedy and reactions to it, increasing in rancor and in condemnation as the tragic truth began steadily revealing itself, from 1941 on.

Moreover, this study endeavors to establish, not only reactions to the tragic results of the Holocaust itself by victims, survivors and outsiders, but also to identify the specific issues preoccupying the writers, how they addressed themselves to them and how they reacted in view of their full realization of the finality of the Holocaust and the futility of it all.

Having exposed the issues within the context of poetic expression, this study seeks also to establish the degree of reaction, particularly in Chapter Five, which intrinsically touches upon the very essence and meaning of Jewish existence in the historical, theological and national framework of reference.

Of particular interest is this study's finding that Hebrew poetry maintains to a large degree that since the Holocaust is beyond explanation, all explanations of traditional theodicy have rendered themselves totally unacceptable, a phenomenon unparalleled heretofore in Hebrew literature and Jewish thought.

And finally, this study also finds, by the admission of the poets themselves, that Hebrew poetry has obviously not yet succeeded in giving full expression to the awesome topic of the Holocaust. It gave only expression of its anguish over the great tragedy and vented its wounded emotions. Ergo, Hebrew poetry still awaits, according to the poet Aharon Zeitlin, Z"L, the great epic to be written . . .

NOTES

1. Rashi, on *Lamentation* Chp. 1:1.
2. Bernfeld, Simon. *Sefer Hadmaot.*
3. Bialik, Ch. N. *Al Hashchitah.*
4. Katzenlson, Yitzchak, *Ktavim Acharonim.*
5. Bossak, Ve'ata Eynay Ra'u.

II

THE STATE OF SHOCK

"Holocaust is coming! . . .
Evil is close by! . . .
Be alert! . . .
Comrade, be on guard! . . .

— *Mordechai Temkin, "Kol Balaylah"*

Never before in our long history of suffering has any tragedy so thoroughly shocked and shattered our people as the Holocaust perpetrated by Nazi Germany. The Nazi engulfment of Europe came at a time when the fruits of the "Spring of Nations" seemed to be ripening. The long awaited fulfillment of the promises of social progress and human equality amidst democratic evolution were slowly emerging on the European continent, not only on the collective level, but in the individual European's awareness. Humanism spread its wings seemingly freeing European society step by step from the fetters of religious prejudice and class struggles, preparing the way toward greater personal freedom in word and deed. Yet, the inbred religious and national discriminations persisted, although in a somewhat more tolerable fashion. Economic difficulties, and social inequalities, fed the flames of collective and personal anti-Semitism, chronic in Eastern Europe. In comparison, Western European anti-Semitism was not as fashionable and was more covert.

Many Jews entertained hopes of becoming politically integrated and culturally Westernized while many more proudly aimed at retaining their authentic Jewishness and national aspirations. Europe's multi nationalistic resurgence was a most didactic lesson for Jewish nationalism. It sparked the hopes of European Jewry for national self-determination in their ancestral homeland. As a consequence, political Zionism, at the turn of the century, became not only popular, but a central force in the national life of European Jewry. Hence, hope and not depression was the password of European Jewry across all its broad diversity and extremities, and in spite of its serious social and economic problems, on the eve of the Nazi onslaught.

With the outbreak of World War Two the true Nazi character was exposed, by virtue of its premeditated and immediate atrocious treatment of Jews collectively, and many non-Jewish intellectuals individually. This unprecedented treatment, far beyond its known behavior since the Nazi takeover in Germany, shocked and paralyzed the Jewish community of Europe across all social, political, religious, and economic strata.

More profound and devastating, however, was the personal shock suffered by individuals. The swift Nazi victory and its resultant terror which was unexpectedly intense and persistent from the outset, allowed no respite to retrench collective positions. The Jews were overnight entrapped in a defenseless position and totally unprepared to cope with the new and frightening situation.

None could adjust somehow, in some way, to the new realities and conditions, and seek ways and means to cope with them or escape from them. For this reason the psychological perplexity caused not only agonizing anxiety, but a collective depression due to sheer helplessness.

European Jews were not suffering from naivete. They were simply mentally unprepared to face collective disaster. They no longer believed that officially organized and sanctioned acts of terror and annihilation were possible. To face total destruction at the hands of Nazi Germany, with the tacit support of a silent and uncooperative Christian collective and no help in sight from the free world, seemed impossible and inconceivable.

In short, the Jewish population was morally and physically incapable of accepting the Nazi reality and it could not absorb the shock of the foreboding signs of imminent destruction.

It would, however, be misleading to assume that no voices were raised in warning before it all happened. There were those who felt profoundly that Europe contained the specter of the destruction of its Jewry in spite of its humanization and liberalization. Among them was the old historian Dr. Bernfeld, who authored the compendium *Sefer Hadmaot* (The Book of Jewish Tears), the story of our martyrology and martyrdom. In summarizing his documented history of Jewish suffering, he wrote almost prophetically: "We are afraid that what may befall us in the future will be more terrible than ever before."

In similar terms, the celebrated Zionist leader Ze'ev Jabotinsky pleaded incessantly with European Jewry in the 1930s: "If you will not liquidate the Galut willingly, it will eventually liquidate you." Thus spake the historians . . .

The poets arrived at the same conclusion, but not through observation of history. They sensed it. Oft times they sounded strange and their words were disdainfully treated as nebulous apocalyptics. Yet, with hindsight, we now know that they spoke like prophets. We are now amazed when we reread the famous verses of the poet Zalman Shneur, written in the days of World War One. He saw Germany then and he sensed the danger that Germany represented. Unfortunately no one took seriously his vision of the approaching horror. This is what he wrote:

The Middle ages are rapidly approaching
Do you hear their steps O man of spirit,
Do you sense the creeping dust
And the distant smell of sulphur?

Like in the wake of a solar eclipse
A silent opppression pervades one's heart,
The earth and the atmosphere.
The Gothic Dark Ages bring fire and brimstone
The medieval crocodile is turning over
To break out of his shell . . .

Just a while longer and he will explode
Destroying cities and gardens.
Breaking the bonds of civilization . . .
And reducing them to scorched chaff . . .

His might will be greater than ever before . . .
Electric fire will he fulminate . . .
And smoke will bellow from his throat . . .
His nostrils exhale murder.

Where will he break his globe-like egg?
No one knows nor can it be predicted.

Does it really matter whether a universally
Dispersed people knows it or not?

Wherever Jews reside,
There disaster will strike them first . . .
The Middle Ages are approaching!

— *"Y'mey Habeynaim Mitkarvim"*

Uri Zvi Greenberg too expressed similar fears in his "Vision of Doom for his People". Yet no one paid much heed. On the contrary, he was despised and denounced like the prophets of yore: " 'He spreads unjustified fear of oncoming destruction upon the wings of poetry' — this was the reaction of his contemporaries and reality repaid them with fierce revenge."[1]

Indeed, the lonely visionaries of the times saw the writing on the wall: "Mene, Mene, Tekel Ufarsin", (*Daniel* V:25) but this time they appeared in bold letters written with blood and fire. And when their predictions came to pass in the most barbaric form that man could have devised, should there be any wonder at the havoc and shock wrought among the Jewish masses?

Thus the poet Yaakov Cahan:

The Holocaust's thunderbolts shocked us,
Its frightening excesses terrified us,
And we were silenced.

We were rendered impotent,
To think or even feel a particle
Of the infernal pangs of a people slaughtered
By the hands of man
In the bright sunlight.

We bowed our heads in mourning
While clandestine fires devoured us.
Man's shame!

Indeed, we are ashamed of mankind.
His superior intellect and spirit embarrass us,
His seventy wisdoms betrayed us,
They turned into nightmares . . .
Indeed, we are ashamed of mankind,

And perplexed about God Himself!
Was it for this the world was created,
And man given understanding,
That he might exceed in wickedness
And wantonly mistreat his brother?
And what of the words of comfort and
Bright dreams of a future world?

— *Shirim*

The Holocaust discredited any confidence in man's ethical power. The idea of man's centrality in the economy of existence was proven disastrous. The theocentric concept which was vacated in order to enthrone the homocentric ideal (a serious attempt to worship man and his materialism), totally collapsed in the crucible of the moral challenge posed by the Holocaust. And irony of ironies! Man's self-deception under the tenuous guise of culture had finally revealed its true moral character. Man in the final analysis failed to be sensitized to the call of ethical responsibility . . . Instead,

The categorical imperative
Raises a knife,
Historical logos
Becomes an executioner;
And Wagner conducts
The butcher-shop orchestra.

— Israel Efros, "Anachnu Hador"

In these few terse phrases the poet philosopher Israel Efros unmasks the German. He unveils the treacherous character of the descendants of the Teutons. Germany, famed for its scientific, cultural, and academic attainments, harnessed these disciplines to the service and support of its obnoxious racial theories, perverted nationalism, and pathological hatred for the Jew, in whose name Nazism was preparing to embark upon a thousand year empire of the pure, Germanic, superior race of "Das Herren Volk."[2]

In view of the aforementioned facts we can more readily appreciate the reasons for the shock to have been so pervasive and persistent on all levels.

Moreover, the rapid transition from utter disbelief in the possibility of annihilation to a realization of its utter certainty, addtionally disoriented the Jewish population and caused further resignation.

It is obvious that poetry's reaction to the shock differed in its intensity no less than that of individual reactions of the people who experienced it in person. Shock has been defined by Professor Fishel Shneurson as "reaction to disasters that go beyond the boundaries of human suffering, until the mind cannot grasp them. When fear overreaches the level of tolerance . . .[3]

Of this difficulty in grasping these feelings, Abraham Shlonsky writes:

> The face of a new day
> That has not yet arrived
> We welcome
> With stuttering syllables.
>
> — "Heykitzuni, Baboker Habaot"

Shneurson elucidates further, explaining that at the onset of shock, two mental illusions are at work. One illusion leads to "celebrating" the tragedy, which contains a sublimity of sorts. No sooner does the impact of the event subside and the "festiveness" of mourning pass, the person begins experiencing the impact of the tragedy in all its naked pain. The pain and hurt become a constant reality which no manner of comfort can assuage.

This was the essence of Michael Deshe's reaction:

> And I don't know whether
> To rend my clothes and eulogize
> A world of beauty and glitter that was,
> And was lost to me forever . . .
> Or should I rather curse and pour out my wrath upon
> This hypocritical and deceptive glory.
> Cursed be the skies of blue,
> Accursed be the sun's brilliance
> For having failed to stop
> Producing its brightness
> On the day of genocide,
> Horror and devastation.
>
> — *"Urim B'lev Yam"*

Moshe Tabenkin's verse reflects with still greater impetus the sense of despair after the initial shock has been absorbed and the setting in of an awareness that no comfort can be found in this terrifying reality.

> Who has the strength to carry day and night
> The constant fear in his heart;
> Of the presence of gallows everywhere in the world . . .
>
> What has happened to our era?
> Like in Gomorrah
> Nightly terror and daily fears . . .
> How did it happen?
> How did our world become a Sodom?
>
> — "Echa Nisa"

Thus speaks the poet. He no longer indulges in any illusions.

His poetry reacts with stark awareness to the tragedy of a shocked and trapped people and its agony. It speaks, although haltingly in the beginning, of the catastrophe and of the state of despair so evident everywhere. It speaks of the loneliness that resulted from the shock and of the prevailing anxiety and helplessness. It speaks of the lost dream, of the shattered hope and of the oppressive thought that there may be no future for him.

> My dream has been smashed on the altar,
> My life is entrapped in sorrow,
> In the twilight my heart hovers
> In the garden of longings.
>
> — "Notarti K'etz Boded"

The second illusion from the shock experience is the one "of the last and shocking doubt." Even though we possess startling documentation of the Holocaust atrocities, nevertheless, for the distant observer, no matter how empathic he may wish to be, this horrifying nightmare remains nebulous and inexplicable. It is imperceptible and inconceivable to the normal mind that all this unbelievable mass murder has really taken place. The moral mind is incapable of accepting this morbid thought regardless of its historic truth.

The aspect of innocent doubt however prevents total despair. This is the general rule: any tragedy that occurs at an unknown distance, as long as one does not witness it in person and some of whose details are by logic or emotion of an uncertain quality, retains the illusion of some doubt. This applies not only to those who were spared the Nazi rod. Even those who were subject to it have had difficulties in accepting the finality of the Final Solution, even in the throes of death, as it actually proved to be so mercilessly final.

Hence the shock aspect of that period's poetic creations contain also reflections of doubt, alarm and perplexity.

I am so frightened
As my vision grows dim
Imagining a Jewish corpse
Dragged out from the mire
Of a dark pit . . .
And nobody knows
What terrors reign within me
While I stroll in leisurely fashion
In the splendor of a blessed day.

— Avraham Broides, *M'adam L'adam*

It is clear that this fear is based on information that can be seen from both sides of the truth. Doubt here was on a rampage as the news of the frightening events reached the ears of the distant poets, who were only able to sublimate their helplessness into a spark of hope and soothe their anguished conscience. Much of this inner wrestling and oppressive remorse find their strongest expression in the personal confessions of the Jewish poets as the news began trickling in about the Nazi terror in all of Europe.

The news of my brethren's death
Pounds incessantly upon my heart
Day and night I envisage
A funeral procession . . .!
En masse do the tortured
Pass me by, leaden eyed.
And while man's eye
Gleams and smiles
I hear them trembling in horror
And flowing tears.

— Hillel Bavli, "Shisha M'elef"

Hebrew poetry's response to the "shock" has also sharply underscored the crippling indifference of a silent world which stood by without lifting a finger.

Asher Barash lamented thus:

My sister was violated,
And my brother was strangled.
My father was thrown alive into the pit.
And my mother expired from pangs of starvation . . .

None can stop sighing,
Nor from questioning refrain
The meaning of existence
That seems to be in vain.

There's no eye that's not tearing . . .
Nor longer do I know
For whom to shed tears
And eulogize in my woe.

— *Tzel Tzoharaim,* "Ein Ish Bocheh"

Shaul Tschernichovsky, who lived long enough to perceive the truth of the Holocaust, reacted with a pained awareness in the poem, "The Murdered of Sirmonia," to his inability to express the tragedy of Jewish martyrology that staggers the human mind. He claims that Jewish martyrdom is beyond poetic expression . . .

There are things
Man cannot hear,
Nor make heard!
Lest he
Lose his sanity.

— Sh. Tschernichovsky, "Harugei Sirmonia"

We began this study with Hebrew poetry's response to the feeling of shock that prevailed at the outset of the Nazi onslaught, or more precisely, how Hebrew poetry expresses the sense of shock. Obviously the roots of the Holocaust's poetic creations are grounded in this feeling of shock, and out of this psychological condition Hebrew poetry derived its mood and mode. The poetic creations of the initial period of the all-out Nazi invasion reflect exploding pent-up emotions, anxiety for our lonely and abandoned people in their desperate and fateful struggle. True to its calling, Hebrew poetry attests to the psychological and spiritual perplexity that prevailed within the Jewish community. There broke forth an outcry over a looming disaster impossible to describe with exactitude, because of its magnitude — the merciless unfolding of the last and final chapter of a thousand-year history of European Jewry.

The poet's desperate outcry of shock and alarm was no less stunning and confusing than that of every Jewish man, woman, and child who experienced the "Shock," but psychologically were unable to adjust to a condition of portentious implications.

NOTES

1. Uri Tzvi Greenberg: "In Malchus Fun Tzelem." See Sulam, Vol. 9, 5713, pgs. 19-21 article by Miriam Atara: "El Keshet Habrit."

2. Leon Poliakov: *Harvest of Hate.*

3. Fishel Shneurson: "Psychologia Shel Shoah U'tkumah" (The Psychology of the Holocaust and Restoration).

III

DESPAIR

Hope has vanished,
Completely disappeared . . .

There is a queue to the gallows
And one for agony . . .

Let's sing the song of despair . . .
On the hangman's sledge
Our flesh is crushed
O Lord of Israel
Who is like unto Thee!?

— Blaustein, "Rachamim V'Dam"

The poetry of despair which emerged from the Ghettos or extermination camps cannot be compared to that which was written by poets outside the Nazi realm as a reaction to the shock trauma. The latter was predominantly reflective and empathic.

> What is despair? Despair is a state of depression characterized by sadness, downheartedness or feelings of indifference to a resignation beyond hope . . ! It is governed by a depressive syndrome which reflects pessimism, discouragement and hopelessness. In despair, one suffers also from delusions in which commonly the person will be prone to express ideas of guilt, unworthiness and self-accusation. Suicidal thoughts are frequently entertained. Tension, fear, anxiety, panic, suspicion, hate, perplexity and irritabilty are symptomatic of despair.
>
> — Noyes and Kolb, *Modern Clinical Psychology*

The father of "logotherapy", Dr. Viktor E. Frankl of Vienna, himself a victim of the Nazi era and a former inmate of Concentration Camps, makes an important observation on the subject:

Despair or disappointment in life is not pathological. Human anguish even in times of despair is not pathological. It is a mental depression but not mental sickness . . . (*Man's Search For Meaning*) This Franklian observation is of great importance to understand the topic on hand as we proceed to delve into the subject of despair as reflected in Hebrew poetry.

Thus writes M.Z. Volfovsky, himself a witness:

> All is shut down around us . . .
> Even an echo won't answer . . .
> Space is entrapped and frozen in its own grief.
> No thunder will roll from the sky; no sound nor cry.
> The pain . . .
> Has been silenced . . .
> Sit down on the ground,
> Carry the burden of your shame in silence,
> Without rebellion, without mockery . . .
>
> — "Ghetto 5703"

In spite of the enormous amount of material that has been written regarding the Holocaust in poetry, essays, stories, diaries, biographies, testimonies, and factual accounts of daily events, very little has been written about the psychology of the persecuted and the psychological state of mind of the doomed to death in the Ghettos and Concentration Camps. Almost alone in this particular area has been the aforementioned Dr. Viktor Frankl, who dealt particularly with man's invincible will to live and his ability to find meaning in life and in living even under the most tragic and desperate conditions.

What happened to the Jew's Diaspora psychology, with it legendary stamina which had conditioned him throughout the generations to face fateful challenges, when the Nazi hordes descended upon him, and he found himself trapped, helpless and encircled with no chance to escape his doom? How did he think and react when suddenly he became totally impoverished with no way of earning a living and at the same time lost his personal dignity as an independent person? What happened to his personal life when he was dispossessed and driven out of his home and deprived of privacy, forced into impossible Ghetto conditions to share, for instance, a room with several families? What happened to the individual under such perplexing social and communal conditions when his uniqueness and personality were instantaneously wiped out in this terrifying confusion?

No authoritative study has yet been made. Some insights can be found in personal accounts and documents which throw some light on the psychological and emotional conditions, attitudes and reactions of the *Shoah* (Holocaust) victims.

The swift Nazi invasion of Eastern Europe and its concomitant brutal impact threw the Jewish populace into a state of despair. At the very beginning, they sensed an organized plan of gradual liquidation at work; what shocked the people was the obvious conspiracy of silence, if not outright cooperation, on the part of the non-Jewish population, which facilitated in time the complete execution of the diabolic German master plan of the "Final Solution." Obviously, it took some time for the Jewish community to regain its collective and individual awareness after this sudden onslaught before resuming the imperative tasks of retaining some semblance of collective care and concern.

In those days, immediately following Nazi occupation, in the initial confusion, a selfish attitude seemed to have prevailed. It seemed to proclaim the Darwinian theory as the axiom of life: the strongest survives. The deceptive illusion that individual survival was possible, in spite of all the signs to the contrary, persisted on the personal level while the collective view was extremely pessimistic. This is why many improprieties were perpetrated within the Jewish community which scandalized many people. The fact is that there were individuals who took advantage of and chose to exploit every opportunity for their own benefit. It was not so much a matter of greed as it was the result of despair: live now because tomorrow we may be dead. . . .

The general conditions were more often than not physically and mentally intolerable. Every waking moment of one's life in the Ghetto was subject to indignities, humiliation, fear and physical abuse. The Nazi-planned overcrowding of the Ghettos created impossible living conditions. The human congestion brought epidemic diseases, squalor, terrible sanitary problems, hunger, despair and resignation. From the social aspect, the tensions of interpersonal relationships were tragically exacerbated. Overnight the differences among social, intellectual and economic strata were wiped out. People were thrown together into the Ghettos where different characters, tempers, educational levels, upbringing and habits were forced into physical proximity. Most devastating was the deprivation of privacy and individuality. In short, this psychological trauma of losing all personal distinctions and social differences contributed in no small degree to the general spiritual depression of the beleaguered Jewish community. The once successful, respected professionals or prosperous businessmen and intellectual elite, were rendered incapable of competing with many other people who were better conditioned to roughing it and more adroit in providing for themselves. In such vulnerable conditions, petty theft, immoral behavior, insensitivity and even acts of brutality, e.g. The Jewish Police, took place. Hence, impossible conditions bred egoism in the name of self preservation for this is what it was all about, possible survival or certain death.

This, in fact, was the Nazi plan: create intolerable conditions in a compact controllable area surrounded by hostile forces. Create oppressive congestion and denigrate the person by various methods of harassment, terror and degrading forced labor. Create a controlled condition of hunger and in time you render the population resigned, hapless, phlegmatic, impotent and incapable of organizing any significant rebellion. Prepare them to accept subconsciously any lie for "supposed" better conditions somewhere else, and this would lead to their submitting themselves for the final annihilation without resistance.[1]

This was only one side of the tragic story. Amidst the aforementioned conditions, there existed also the indestructible Jewish spirit and the human will to survive. Actually, in spite of these awful conditions, had the Nazis left them in the Ghettos, the great majority of European Jewry would have surely survived. The fact remains that the unavoidable internal abuses were perpetrated by relatively small numbers. The great majority of people did not lose their dignity nor their human and humane perspective on life.

We ought also to remember, that the Ghetto inmate had to contend with a dual struggle, namely: with the Nazi henchman and his collaborators waiting for him outside and with an instinctive human desire to live and give some sort of existential meaning to life, in spite of the impossible conditions, the awareness of the cruelty of a silent world, and the forebodings of an impending doom.

In retrospect, even the most righteous of men, the mentally strongest and physically most resilient, were not expected to meet as gallantly these persistent daily challenges of mental anguish and physical terror as the Jewish collective did indeed meet and endure. In fact, no sooner were the initial shocks of persecutions, intimidations, expulsions and ghettoization over and some mental adjustments made, when a new awareness pervaded the Jewish population. All realized that the terrifying lot was shared by the entire community and there were no exceptions nor escape from it. The old Judaic ethical guiding concept that "all Israel is responsible for one another" received new meaning and became the most aspiring ideal of Jewish solidarity. Great heroism, devotion and sacrifice took place. People risked their own lives to help save others. Often there were some opportunities, especially for younger people, to escape the Ghetto. Yet most of them remained, sharing the doleful lot of the community and family. Jewish inventiveness, self-aid as well as religious and cultural activities continued to the very last moment. Yes they could have survived in spite of it all . . .

From this synoptic review of the morbid aspects of the Ghetto conditions, we can anticipate poetry's particular sensitivity to the state of despair that was dominant across all social levels and ages.

In our Ghetto it's so bitter and bad,
Every rifle shot drives us mad.
In every corner guards are found,
Like thieves and criminals,
We're kicked around.
With every passing day,
The burden gets heavier in our way . . .
What will be tomorrow?
Who can say? Know?
Double the suffering,
Twice the woe?

— "Bageto Shelanu," *Prager Anthology*

The very question: "What will be tomorrow?" when it is posed by a mature person amidst hunger pangs and spiritual and mental anguish certainly reflects in him a pervasive sense of despair. How much more urgent and shattering are similar questions when they are asked in all the innocence by a desperate young girl?

Oh, mother. Why did you give birth to me
And bring me into this world,

To give me the name of "Jew"
And to hand me over to my Jewish fate? . . .

They gather us into the stadium . . .
Precious things they take from us.
With some they populate concentration camps,
But others they take to be shot . . .

On the way to execution-place,
I was able to ransom myself,
I rescued my life from the gallows
To be in this accursed trap once again . . .

— "Hoi, Lama, Ima Y'liditini," *Prager Anthology*

Yet the instinct to live remained persistently strong throughout the Holocaust nightmare. Actually, the will to survive helped in fact overcome many unbearable ordeals. Nevertheless, who can dare perceive the tragedy of a father whose child was murdered before his eyes or that of a despairing hunger-stricken mother imprisoned in the Ghetto, helpless to provide any comfort for her child. How moving are these desperate words:

Listen, my child, the winds are moaning.
Close your eyes and sleep.
They have taken away your father,
Where, I do not know.

Alone, with you, we are left in the world.
This calamity frightens me so.
Seven we were altogether,
Now, we are two and no more . . .

The night is long and stormy.
In the house . . .
Not a crumb of bread,
Torn are your shoes, my baby,
Rest your weary head . . .

Hear me, my child
It's forbidden to cry,
Here a sentry walks his rounds,
He'll shoot at will,

Just for the thrill,
Any possible Jewish passerby.

— "Sh'ma Yaldi," *Prager Anthology*

"The Nocturnal Fears", by M. Gebirtig, mirrors in verse the tragic psychology of fear in the Ghetto and records the indelible impact on Jews living under the constant threat of death:

Like walking upon a sand path,
So trudge the tired slaves.
The cumbersome Ghetto days
Drag on . . .
No less do the sleepless nights.

The lingering hours are heavier than lead,
Every moment awful and full of dread.
We pray the day will soon take flight,
And peace replace the darkness of night.

We cannot sleep, only the ear is attuned
Whose door will be squeaking from entry at night
While our hearts shudder from terror's might . . .

A terrible thought suddenly crosses our mind,
The enemy must be lurking in nocturnal blight,
To seal a Jew's fate during the night
To slake his bloodthirsty appetite . . .

So great are our fears that our very limbs freeze
At the sound of the wind rustling through leaves.

In the silence of the nights
We bid farewell to our wives,
Our mothers, children and friends.
Humiliated like slaves we lie terrified on our beds
And that's the story of our sleepless nights.

— "Biutei-Laylah," *Prager Anthology*

At times, when the suffering in the Ghettos became unbearable, some ventured to envy the dead, for they had been freed from further agony:

The Ghetto is quiet, barbed wire shut tight
So too is the graveyard late at night
The Ghetto dwellers, pale, wan slaves,
Stand in rows, like stones at graves
The cemetery is busy as a fair
Grave diggers worn out from burying there
Those liberated from the Ghetto prison
Death, has broken their chains,
Free from here on from lingering pains.

— "Sheket Bageto," *Prager Anthology*

Yet the mental anguish was much greater than the physical one. The Ghetto was like a prison overcrowded and encircled. Its physical layout was generally in accordance with the Nazi plan, intentionally situated in center of town, surrounded by a predominantly inhospitable, anti-Semitic population who tantalized, in a way, the ghettoized Jews by their freedom of movement. This was an additional demoralizing mental torture which contributed to depression and indescribable humiliation:

At times, in a grey, gloomy hour of the day,
I take a peek through the window of my Ghetto prison,
How outside of the Ghetto walls . . .
The wheel of life is turning . . .

I stand and gaze at the outside world,
And everything looks normal from here . . .
Nothing seems to have changed in the world,
Only the Jew's life within the Ghetto walls,
Is sealed for doom and the pyre . . .

Why has a tiny little ant or worm,
A place reserved on earth?
But I a Jew for no crime or sin,
Am ostracized, and cursed and forlorn . . .

— Adela Fruchtman, "Mib'ad Lachalon Hageto"

The frustration of the Ghetto inmate was the more unbearable since he was cruelly afforded the opportunity to be made aware of his Jewish fate to be so much different from the rest of mankind. From the Ghetto window he perceived that nothing had really changed.

The world had not left its normal orbit. The globe had not collapsed nor had nature gone astray. Only the Jew was denied the right to live in it. Only one recourse seemed to have been left for him, to bemoan his fate. But what was one to do when one ran out of tears?

Why does my heart ache and I cannot weep?
And so somber is my life . . .

Why does not the sun shine on me,
To warm my emaciated body?
For neither raiment nor shoe do I have,
To cover my nakedness!

Is it true that I no longer have a father?
And my mother is missing too?
Where are you brothers and sisters?
Is anyone of you still alive?

Why don't I have any tears to cry
To bitterly bewail my lot?
And Kaddish I should be saying aloud
For my father and mother and for all!

— M. Shenker, "Halev Nilchatz"

The author here reflects no hope. He speculates in his despair whether anyone has survived the deportations, rendering him a mourner obligated to recite the Kaddish. This, in fact, reflected the predominant Ghetto mood. Life in the ebbing days of the Ghetto was lived in a limbo, a day at a time. Life eventually became stagnant and resigned, a sort of suspended animation. There remained only enough heartbeat to help one resignedly respond to the Gestapo order to line up for the last march or transport from which most did not return.

Are there many more days left?
The heart does not predict anything good —
Right now it's so bad, so bad
My hands are heavy and my feet I drag.
As if in deep dark mud
All existence has been halted.
It may be the last fleeting hour for us . . .

So broken up, forlorn and poor
Not even a glimmer of revenge is left.
In this desperate hour I pray to my God:
O Lord, give me strength
I beseech Thee I need it so much.

— Jacques Gordon, "Ha'od Nisharu Lanu Yamim Harbe"

In spite of the gnawing despair, and the awful reality that seemed to extinguish any hope, a spark of hope remained deeply imbedded in the psyche of the people.

I want to live,
I cannot die just yet . . .
I want to reach the happy time,
To see my persecuted people free.

— Yasha Rabinowitz, "Hatzavaa"

This aspect of holding on to the spirit of hope, no matter how dimmed and weak it appeared to be, has also been reflected in the collective behavior of retaining a standard of "Mentschlichkeit" notwithstanding the abuses that existed within the community.

Hillel Zeitlin, replying to one of the "Oneg-Shabbat" questionnaries by the Ringelblum Group in the Warsaw Ghetto, made the following observation: "Had there been a concentration of four hundred thousand people of other nations, in such inhuman congestion, it is very questionable whether they could have maintained, under similar conditions, such a high moral standard and social responsibility as the Jews did . . ."[2]

As mentioned, the Ghetto was not spared from beholding the rise of a Jewish Ghetto hierarchy of haughty persons and petty tyrants who were chosen by the Nazis to administer its internal affairs. Besides the Jewish "police," the Judenrat received at best a dubious rating.[3] The story of the Lodz Ghetto and its "Jewish King" Rumkovsky is a well recorded tragic story. This is how Rumkovsky was sarcastically perceived in verse (punning on the name Chayim Rumkovsky, "Chayim" meaning life):

The Jews were . . .
Inscribed for life and not for death,

Chaim Rumkovsky is our Master
He performs daily miracles,
With cries and rants.
Chaim Rumkovsky,
Our daily life sustains,
By distributing crumbs of bread
To whomever he likes.

— "Chayim Shelanu," *Prager Anthology*

Not all Ghetto leaders acted like Rumkovsky. In the Ringelblum documents and in *The Scroll of Agony* by Chayim Kaplan, Adam Czerniakow of the Warsaw Ghetto is remembered as a hero and martyr. He refused to provide daily lists to the Gestapo of ten thousand names for "Transports" to death. Instead, he committed suicide rather than become an involuntary accomplice in this heinous crime.

Serious literary discussion regarding suicide took place in Goethe's times. After the Shoah, a similar discussion ensued as to whether there was heroism in death or in the struggle for survival in spite of the impossible conditions. Clearly, this was not a belleteristic discussion for public consumption. It has been, however, a controversial issue that still continues to plague students of the Holocaust.

The question that is posed is as follows: should only those who died either on the gallows, in the gas chambers, at mass executions, with the partisans, underground, in revolts and by suicide be considered martyrs, or do those who struggled, suffered and fought and somehow survived deserve too to be awarded the martyr's status? Who will in fact dare to judge?[4]

The history of the Holocaust has already made its verdict known. Both the dead and the survivors have received this status. However, all who died and no matter where they met their death, will be remembered as the martyrs of the Holocaust.

In the history of mankind we have a rich heritage of myths surrounding the death of martyrs. Martyrdom was always seen as an act of great heroism. Consequently, national myths of heroism and martyrdom were created and have inspired the people. Yet upon closer analysis, the heroic stories did not always reflect true martyrdom although they may have been rooted in some true facts. Hence, for example, the story of the "Ninety three maidens" who supposedly committed suicide rather than serve as prostitutes for the Nazi soldiers (Hillel Bavli, Yehudah Karni, Abraham Broides, David Shimoni and Mordecai Tabenkin wrote on the subject), and the dramatic monologue of Yosl Rakover (a Tzvi Kolitsch invention) serve as classic examples of myths of heroism spun from the tragedy of the Shoah.

Yitzchak Katzenelson is the tragic eulogizer of Warsaw Jewry's *churban*/annihilation. His authentic account of the pervading despair immortalizes the total mood of resignation that dominated the life in the Warsaw Ghetto from the very outstart until the very end with the infamous "selections". His epic reflects two rudimentary aspects: the tragedy in the fact that there was no way out and that all were doomed to die; secondly, and more distressing was the other fact, as he saw it, that there was no meaning even to "Kiddush Hashem," to the act of martyrdom. He went as far as denying particularly Cherniakov a martyr's death. He claimed that Czerniakow died out of despair rather than in an act of protest against the impending cruel annihilation of Warsaw's Jewry.

Czerniakow? . . .
Why are you crying?
After all — you are a decent fellow . . .
Yet let's not forget:
Your Jewishness was miniscule.
Was the daily delivery of ten thousand Jews too much?
And six thousand would have been acceptable?
You are angry — at whom?
At yourself?
For this reason you're beating your breast
And saying: "Al-Chet"! . . .

Adam — you have chosen the bitter potion to swallow
And bring an end to it all . . .
But the Jew in the Ghetto —
Him they kill . . .
There is more courage to be killed . . . you know!
Never mind — you drink poison
And try to scrape your record clean . . .

I swear, indeed, on the very brink of your conversion —

You gave meaning and paid a price
For your Jewish demise . . .

— "The Song of the Slaughtered Jewish People," Chp. 5

Every trouble has its own time, every pain its own reason and every despair its significance. The despair that enveloped the Jewish populace reached its climax at the end of the first two years of Nazi atrocities. By then, despair was no longer grounded in the unknown factor. Too much was already known and there is no justification for the sometimes heard claim that the facts were totally unknown. Much information was daily arriving with detailed accounts of the systematic liquidations of Ghetto after Ghetto. By the early summer of 1942 even details regarding the deported and their lot began trickling in with greater frequency almost daily.

The people are loaded
Into train cars like preserves
Indeed, know well
Where they are taken . . .

— Rilke Glazen, "Karon Hamavet," *Prager Anthology*

Katzenelson's poem corroborates this sad truth about the people's knowledge of the tragic fate that awaited them. In words dripping, literally, with blood, we read the desperate story of a people at the world's dead-end whom no one cared to help . . .

Woe unto me, for I knew,
And so did my neighbors
All of us, every Jew . . .

Silent, each person afraid of himself,
We kept our thoughts muted,
And our voices within . . .

We knew it before the Nazi hoodlums came,
Long before the Ghetto shame,
Much before the Concentration Camps:
Before Chelmno, Belzec, Ponari:
The infamous stations of our bitter end . . .

At the early days of the Nazi war

I recall . . .
When we met a distant friend,
Instead of looking into each other's eyes
We squeezed each other's hand . . .

Not a whisper nor a gaze,
The eyes feared to look in one's face.
By glimpses or a hand shake,
Our inner thoughts were disclosed.
What the invisible words meant on the walls . . .
Tekel, Tekel . . .

We all knew and the Gentiles too,
Murdered everywhere will be every Jew.
Without a rhyme, a reason or clue.

The die has been cast
An irreversible law:
To destroy the Household of Israel
At the pleasure of the Nazi foe . . .

— Y. Katzenelson, *op. cit.,* Chap. 7

The scathing rebuke, "without a rhyme or reason," provides for us the key to the oppressive mental anguish and spiritual despair of the ghettoized Jews.

The Jews were concentrated into the Ghettos and so manipulated psychologically and physically that it became impossible to find a way out. When the people realized the trap they were in, and began searching for avenues of escape, it was too late . . . All roads out of the Ghetto were closed. The outside Gentile population, unsympathetic to the Jews' plight, would not have been of much help even under more benign conditions, barring some rare humane exceptions. The fact that they were also under an incessant Nazi barrage of intimidation and subject to severe punshiment for abetting in the slightest the concealment or escape of Ghetto Jews finalized the encirclement. Thus, only one road was open for sure, the path to death. When finally the scattered Ghetto revolts broke out, they were very late, too late to be sure, and not predicated upon any hope of preventing the further destruction of the surviving Ghetto remenants. Not at all. It was a gallant attempt of a last desperate act of Samson-like resistance — to die a martyr's death, together with the Nazi predators.

Despair and its inherent silent heroism has many faces. In the poem that follows, we find an all-inclusive expression of the sort of martyrdom, so characteristic of classical Jewish heroism. It is an unparalleled heroism which reflects the anguish of despair amidst profound faith by the very heroes who chose silent death as a means of supreme protest.

In the ruins of an old synagogue chapel,
Lies an old man like a bundle of bones
Rolled up in the parchment of Torah scrolls,
and fasts . . .
The stilled day — light hangs like a towel on a hinge
And for his tardy guest he daily waits with a painful cringe.

A Talit at his feet and a Menorah at the head,
Which reflects the glittering sunset,
As the old man lies with bleeding hands
That once ornamented Torah letter crowns.
But this time he sealed his Torah script
With the blood of his heart in a self made crypt . . .

I brought him daily his morsel of bread
And implored him to say a word or two . . .
But the old man's word was sealed for me
So was his name sworn to secrecy.
Daily I tended to his supposed need,
Yet his morsel remained, for he refused to eat.
His lips were shrivelled like mushrooms at best,
He clung to the parchment like to a mother's breast.
Each step when he heard, his heart awoke
Because for death did he seem to hope.

He never did gaze at me;
To isolate himself from humankind.
From fasting his flesh melted like wax.
As he waited for his eternal peace.
He wrapped his cleansed body in the Torah Scroll
And he for whom he lay in wait
Approached so slowly as if in a crawl . . .

And again I would bring him just a drink,

And place a piece of bread without a blink.
The same as yesterday his emaciated hand,
Seemed to refuse to touch a thing.
I see generations of agonizing Jews
Passing through his body and his sinews,
Carving out their last Testament
On the wall by the moon's glow in the firmament.

But once I tore the parchment from off his head,
And pleaded with him to eat lest he be dead,
This only time he granted me a reply
For his stubborn attitude and why:
Should I take something from this cruel world and enjoy,
May it rather go up in flames and be forever destroyed
With its hypocritical goodness and joy.

On the morrow as the radiance of the sunset spark
Bounced off the Menorah so glintingly stark,
Himself enwrapped in the Torah Scroll
The old man vanished in the letters of the parchment roll.

— "BaKloiz Shenecherav," *Prager Anthology*

In silence of personal and collective suffering and pangs, hunger has been sublimated into a religious fast. The Jew's soul often departed with sacrificial purity from out of the heap of tattered Torah Scrolls which were defiled and desecrated by the abominable Germanic hands.

Hence, the Jew's Talit at his feet and the Menorah at his head . . . Thus perished entire holy communities of European Jews, their leaders marching proudly and undaunted in the front line with a sense of heroic defiance that sprang not so much from their disappointment in God as from their loss of faith in man.

Nevertheless, one ought not assume that the practice of supreme stoicism was characteristic of the Jewish masses in the face of extermination. Nor ought we surmise that the murdered died with a sense of total surrender to God's verdict. Not at all. The human will to live was too strong. Therefore, those last moments of tragic awareness that the end was at hand, have registered shattering anguish beyond description. Those preparations for the foreboding departure and the inner struggle of despair when they all marched together and, in spite of the flickering hope of survival, knew that the end had come; that they were marching on the road of no return. Who can ever recapture these last moments except where this final desperate shriek of protest still reverberates in the conscience of those whose souls have been sensitized by the supreme tragedy of recorded history.

All during the Ghetto period there were expressions envying the dead, and such oft pointed questions as:

> Be honest and ask yourself
> Who is luckier
> We or they?
> We who are still alive
> Or the victims with blood
> Paid already for their lives? . . .
>
> — *Prager Anthology*

However, relatively speaking, few among the Eastern European Jews showed signs of suicide. On the heels of the final Ghetto liquidations as the transportation schedules were proclaimed, a marked last minute increase in suicides took place.

The poet Tzvi Nesher immortalized in one of his poems a characteristic episode reflecting the aspect of suicide as an accepted escape when the end was at hand.

> Many in the Ghetto commit suicide.
> In the street of the Ghetto
> A young boy peddles cyanide.
>
> Cyanide, people, you ought to buy
> A practical item for everyone to try.
> Better painlessly your foe defy
> Than from torture to die.
>
> O you human mortals
> Buy your cyanide potions.
> Compassionately will it by you abide,
> On the day of genocide.
>
> Suddenly, in the midst of his song he stops,
> In painful silence trapped.
> He turns here and turns there.
> Cyanide is not sold anywhere.

Thus stands the pale young merchant,
Dumbfounded in the street,
Himself to some cyanide
He forgot to treat.

— "Shirim MiKiryat Mavet"

And thus the dreaded "deportation" caught up with everyone. The *Umschlagplatz* confusion, the hurried boarding of the train, the last train ride in the "wagon of death" had begun as the locomotive jerked with all its power and the wheels began turning forward . . . Those of us survivors, who experienced that last train ride with our families and friends, will never forget it. Who can forget those anxiety filled days and hours? For most, this was the final ride from the land of the living to the gas chambers and the inferno of the crematoria. This was the trip of no return. In these train cars, the last act of ultimate confrontation and farewell to life and loved ones unveiled itself in all its cruel reality. The torture of the emotional anguish can never be truly recaptured in words:

In the hearts of the condemned on the train,
The wagons great tragedies claim.
Shattering they seem each one to be
And deeper, much deeper than
The depths of the sea.
They cry out, "Save us!" their refrain
"A drop of poison," is their plea.

Mothers clutch their children
Hold them close to their heart,
Kiss them over and over
Knowing they soon must part.

I too am here with my mother alone,
So closely she presses my body to her own,
And I also cuddle up to her.
I sense too well our end is near.

— Rilke Glazen, "Karon Hamavet," *Prager Anthology*

In a similar view we read the following verses permeated with untold despair and anxiety:

And in the wagons of death I go berserk
Between the bitter grave and limitless love.
How strange is our cry of disaster . . .
Whilst the sun shines so splendidly!
My heart be strong and courageous!
To embrace the dead and dear corpses
Perhaps it will warm up my body
Consumed by chill of death
Perhaps the Messiah will warm up!
In the cacophony — the lament rises
In anguish and anger . . .
Why does my heart cry for the golden sun
Which has been befouled by the stench of the dead?
And the train cars speed towards the shores
Of the dreaming lagoon . . .
Like a nocturnal vision . . .
How strange is the road, like a nightmare,
No man sees nor hears!

— Y. Luria, "Even M'kir Tizak"

From the crematoria no poetic verse came back to us. There everything was silenced forever. Never will we know the feelings, despair and anguish that took place in the gas-chamber, in that eternal moment before lives were snuffed out, choked by the deadly gasses, burned on the pyres or bleeding to death in the mass graves.

Those who were selected for slave labor in the Concentration Camps and to an agonizing slow death, left behind but little material in the written form reflecting the immediate reaction to the new reality of torture, suffering, hunger and distress beyond normal human comprehension. Most of the known materials on the Concentration Camp experience are survivors' recollections of the living inferno. They are not of the same emotional intensity as the immediate reactions to experiences that took place before their eyes recorded in the Ghettos or labor camps.

The following is an extant poem, one of the few written by a "Katzetnik" (adjective for a Concentration Camp inmate), reflecting the life of one suspended between life and death:

Hearken my soul, refrain from bemoaning your youth,
A fleeting moment may render valueless the thing you know.
The dawn invites to open your eyes to enjoy . . .

The sight of the hanged or those that were shot.

All people look alike, inextricable from the night,
They plant their shrieks, within the rim of their lips . . .
The mouths have lost their speech,
And the hands tremble . . .

Eyes rise from out the night
To sense the whisper of silence.
And perhaps to answer the question
That breaks forth from the barbed-wire,
Eyes so baffling
Like a message which has never arrived.

— David Sando, "Mileilot B'Mahaneh Hesger"

From the verses of these condemned to annihilation, we derive a clearer insight into the personal tragedy of each victim apart from the collective fate that befell European Jewry.

Another aspect of the poetry-of-despair ought now be examined based upon recollections and reflections of past experiences intrinsically eulogistic, since they were written with a sense of urgency and perhaps subconscious guilt. This poetry deals with the same theme of despair but reflects a much deeper bitterness. These poets wrote not under the influence of anguishing conditions. They wrote under the burden of memories of the past tragedy of a destroyed people which they themselves witnessed indirectly in all its horror.

It need be also emphasized that there is a characteristic difference between the two approaches to the poetry-of-despair in spite of their common denominator.

The expression of despair coming from the Ghetto was essentially an expression of pain and anguish. In most cases it is not argumentative nor critical, confessional nor accusatory, challenging God, man or history. It echoes the intimate tragedy that befell the people and its content is rather inclined to report what has happened, the way it happened and the reaction to what happened. It was written with premeditation, for posterity to know what transpired in those bloody days of Nazi atrocities in the homes, in the streets, in the camps and in the railroad cars on the way to death.

The most impressive poetry on this subject is the aforementioned epic poem by Yitzchak Katzenelson and in no lesser degree the great poem by Meir Bosak. Katzenelson immortalized in his epic, the essence of the *Shoah* (Holocaust). On the basis of this epic alone one can compose the history of the extermination of Polish Jewry. On the other hand, one finds in its reflectiveness a strong tendency to vent one's emotions and sorrow. Therefore, we should not evaluate this poetic material from its artistic aspect but rather from the spirit and mood in which it was then written. One must perceive its desperate tone, conscious and subconscious, particularly when the truth and scope of the cruelty of the annihilation has revealed itself to the poet and the way he reacts emotionally to it from inner despair.

Thus does the poet Elchanan Indelman involve us in his personal sorrow, which is actually our collective grief as he mourns the loss of his and our sisters and brothers. In his poem "My Sister" he tells us of discovering his sister through one of the Ghetto photographs: her face seemed to be full of both hope and despair . . . and he breaks out in a bitter cry:

"Why haven't you been spared, my sister Ruchamah?"

Our private despair which is derived from our personal pain continues to involve us all as if we all are participants in our collective despair as much as entertaining a glimmer of hope, perchance someone survived:

I seek my brothers.
My brothers,
Choked by gas, immolated by fire
My brothers I seek
In the fields and in the meadows,
In the valleys
On the mountains
And in the plains.
I ask the wind in the field:
Have you seen my brothers' ashes . . .
I ask the cloud in the sky
Have you seen my brothers' tears:
In the showers fall
Or in the dew mist?
I asked the morning star
Have you seen my brothers' souls
Among the shining stars
In the heavens high?
I asked the rainbow

Have you seen God
Where He bewails,
Where He cries and sighs
Over the rivers of blood
And His throne rolls
In the dust of human ashes?
Have you seen Him?
Tell God:
I look for my brothers
In fire and in water
In the soft ground
And in the wind;
In the furrowed earth
And in the poem
That may never be forgotten.

— Elchanan Indelman, "Et Achai Ani Mevakesh"

The sacred blood of our people cries out from these personal verses, for the essence of the grief and suffering is over the loss of our people. Much can be reconstructed, restored or even compensated for. But there is no compensation or substitution for the loss of six million individuals. We may, in time, reproduce and close the numerical gap, but we shall never replace those Jews who represented a world of tradition and erudition that was annihilated by the hands of the Nazis and their collaborators. For this very painful reason of our irreplaceable loss, we do not tire of seeking our brothers and sisters in spite of the fact that we have despaired of ever findng them . . .

Where are you, Jewish communities, Holy Congregations
of the European Exile?
Where are you, Sabbath, Holiday and weekday Jews?
Where are you, Jewish children, babies and pupils?
Where are you, saintly Jews, attired with
The beauty of holiness of your Talit and Tephillin?

Where are you, Jews, the dreamers of redemption
And messianic contemplators?
Faithful Jews, whose belief was stronger than death!
Simple Jews, Jews who recited Psalms
And studied holy books,

Jews of grinding poverty,
Who with dignity eked out a living?

Where are you? Where are you "Kol-Nidre"
And "Unesane Tokef" Jews?
"Simchat Torah" Jews, who prayed for the coming
Of the Messiah?
Woe, communities of holy and pure ones, purged
Through suffering,
Whose bread of sorrow and wine of joy
Were mixed with tears?

Jews of Talmudic discourse, giants of Torah learning
And Chassidic devotion.
Jews who endeavored to put the world aright,
Pure hearted and of spiritual elation.
Jews who saved pennies to pay their children's
School tuition,
Jews whose benevolent charity was pure and complete.

Alas, present yourselves and stand up,
All of you, you holy congregation,
The entire people, men and women,
Boys and girls pure of eye and heart.
Dress up in you Shabbes Kapotes,
Elegant or patched,
Dear Jews, whose lustre was as the brightness of
the firmament,
Without a speck or a flaw.

Stand up as one, the way you stood at Sinai
In that awesome dawn of Divine splendor!
Awake and arise to avenge the humiliation of your honor,
For a slaughtered people,
To roar before the roar of anguish is choked
Or consumed in the fire!
Demand justice!
Implore, cry out to the God of Justice, O Lord,
"Do not murder!"

Will you appear? At least once more in your roaring
And thundering voice,
On this defiled earth which has soaked up your blood

To utter intoxication?
This earth which absorbed the marrow of your bones
As if you were never formed out of it . . .
Like a step-mother who denied knowing you
On the day of wrath and anger!

Your ashes are spread over every clod of earth
Indeed over its inner bowels.
The paleness of your faces is reflected in its whiteness
Your scarlet blood reddens every flower
And the atmosphere is permeated with your holy speech
And saturated with your breath.
Your silent roar reverberates in every cry
And in every aching heart.

Woe unto the generation that beheld this annihilation
Which has marched in the parade of suffering
And drained to the dregs the cup of sorrow.
A generation that waited for a miracle that never came
Whose hope turned to naught on the day of disaster and tragedy.
A generation that will carry its tragedy
To the grave, until the bitter end.

— Reuven Weintroib, "Ayeychem?"

Three primary operational bases were central to the Nazi scheme in the annihilation of European Jewry. A) The Ghetto enclaves; B) The Concentration Camps and the semicivilian slave labor units; and C) Annihilation areas such as gas chambers, crematoria, vans, and mass graves in ravines, forests and open pits.

To begin with the last-mentioned first, in these annihilation areas the Germanic murderers and their collaborators played to the last note their grand cannibalistic symphony in the theatre of death. No message ever came back from there. The victims died there either with faith or with blasphemy, in hope or despair. No one will ever know — they took this secret with them forever.

The Concentration Camps were the laboratories of slow death once the victim entered its gates. All hope was lost, as in the message at the gates of Dante's "Inferno":

Per me si va ne la citta dolente;
Per me si va ne l'eterno dolore . . .

Lasciate ogni speranza, voi ch'entrate.

— Canto III

(Through me is the way into the doleful city/ . . . Through me the way into eternal pain/ . . . Abandon all hope, ye who enter . . ./) Auschwitz, Birkenau, Maidanek, Treblinka, Chelmno, Belzec, Dachau, Bergen Belsen, Buna and Odruf, and others were places where every perspective of reality dissipated into nothingness. Human values were crushed and drowned in a bloody whirlpool.

Orphaned, widowed, bewildered and desperate the inmate was left only with the certainty of a tortured existence and death. Either the animalistic instinct to survive or "The Will To Live" enabled the victim to prolong his agony for sometime. As Eli Wiesel observed: in Auschwitz not only the human being was doomed to premeditated extinction, but also the entire matter of humanity was annihilated there. There life was totally emptied of its meaning. Only the Satan ruled there. In Auschwitz, the world lost its heart and soul.

The Concentration Camps will be remembered as the torture chambers where no room to think remained. There the victim was stricken, at the outset of his arrival, with mental paralysis. To think of one's existence was rediculous, and of one's possible survival — absurd. There one's lot was sealed. The only question that persisted was: When will the end come? Yes, the "Katzets" (Abbreviation for Concentration Camps) will be remembered for their dehumanization, terror, infernal torture, starvation and suffering. German ingenuity achieved a human bestiality far beyond Dantian imagination. The camps will be remembered in the tatooes on our arms, in the scars on our bodies and in the lingering inner anguish of a survivor's soul. These indelible experiences are imponderably painful to relate.

But the Ghetto, in spite of its horrible and oppressive conditions, will be remembered as our last loving nest of family togetherness in our struggle with hope and despair. Being together within the family unit, one derived the succor and support, spiritually and morally to sustain oneself in the face of the trauma of hunger, disease, humiliation and deprivation. All that really mattered in those tense and foreboding days was that we were together with our family. The comfort of assurance, a shoulder to cry on, a moment to share, a mother's gentle hand to wipe off a tear . . .

As long as we remained together in the Ghetto, collective suffering was somehow bearable. Even survival we deemed feasible had the Nazis left us in the Ghetto to our own.

For this reason when the awareness of being deported to possible death finally reached the large masses, the ensuing months and weeks of waiting were of immense psychological torture. For this reason the Ghetto memories are more vivid and painful to the survivors. The pesonal tragedies we witnessed; the recalling those moments of separation; the tears that one still sees rolling down the faces of our loved ones; the echo of their voices still reverberates in our hearts and minds. The last parting words: "If we live, we shall meet again . . ." The last hug and kiss. The last embrace, the last moment before being separated forever . . . left an indelible stamp on those who survived. This is why the Ghetto will be remembered and the pain of memory will linger on and hold the survivor in its grip, never to be forgotten.

I shall never forget you, Ghetto, never!
The tone of your song reverberates in "Eichah"
This is your heartfelt and soothing song.
This is your sorrow so dear and profound.
I see your tears, your prayer I hear:
What will happen to the far and the near?
In your streets I feel so pained,
Among your inmates I'm so bitter.
And though my heart aches for you
Everything within you is so beloved to me.
I shall never forget you, Ghetto, never!

— "Lo Eshkachech Haghetto La'ad," *Prager Anthology*

Here the captives quivered from vicious hate,
Here they offered their anxious suppliant prayers,
Here every corner the cry of our tortures contains . . .
And every dilapidated room and hall,
Is permeated with tears like the Wailing Wall.

Who among you foresaw the "Churban" coming?
Who thought this tragedy would come to be?
The voice of the oppressed is rising to Heaven,
Of their tragedy man will hear unto eternity!

Remember forever, my soul, the suburb of the city
Where secrets of Hell were revealed to thee.

Drink to the last drop the cup of accursed poison,
And don't heed the sweetness of peace.

— Y. Chelmsky, "Geto Riga"

And so we move from vivid memories of personal Ghetto experiences to threnody. Indeed, the tragedy of the Ghetto as a Ghetto has spawned its own legend. The oppressive dimensions of the Ghetto and the scope of its psychological degradation corresponded to the Nazi conception of the Ghetto as a preparatory station where the psychological war was to be won first over the population. Deadening any resistance was thus secured through a prolonged degradation and starvation process of the Ghetto dwellers, rendering them easy prey in the concluding stages of the Final Soluton. This is why the Ghetto under the Nazis was uniquely tragic and exclusively Jewish and its dimensions of destruction were often termed as the *Third Churban* of the Jewish people.

Hence, perhaps the Ghetto could only be described in terms of a legend. For only in this sense could it be understood, since its tragic reality defied the heart, mind and pen of a rational human being. Who, except those who personally witnessed it, could ever believe this premeditated and scientifically planned inhumanity of man to man?

This Ghetto legend was in anguish recorded
With scalding tears and dripping blood
In the fading moments of an ebbing life.
Ashamed on the pavement
You lay now demolished
The blood so silent, the tear so cold.

You were recorded during fires . . .
Hands described you,
While losing their pulse;
Mouths whispered you,
While gagged with earth.

There is no legend
As sorrowful as you . . .
Is there an expression adequate enough . . .
To describe your dejection and sorrow? . . .

Here is the Ghetto legend . . .
A dolorous tune,
A melody collapsing
At every crossroad
Under the weight of its grief.
Lonely is the melody
And succor it does not bring,
Jewish pain cannot be assuaged
For the murder of brothers in the Germanic rage.

I shall errect you a rampart
Dying legend . . .
Of all the legends . . .
The most wretched you are . . .
In you the anger is fermenting evermore
Yet compassion within you overflows.
Silently sobbing relentlessly you mourn
Like that mother who has lost her firstborn.

— "Mima'amakim," Author Unknown,
Nasza Tribuna, 1945

There are many professional and dilettante writers and poets who ventured into the Holocaust theme and made their respective contributions to this ever growing literature. But none can match the value and feeling of the authentic message received from the eye-witnesses. No matter how brilliant the writer may be, the *Shoah* subject and its testimony are a literary *sui generis.* To write with understanding and literary skill is not enough. The Holocaust literature was intended to be the repository of authentic eye-witness reports, reactions and the story of Holocaust experiences. Those who have perished and those who have survived wished to record their story and their interpretations of the events for the sake of giving testimony as to the factual tragedy and its imperative lesson unto future generations. The *Shoah* literature, therefore, is expected to be consciously subjective and from this source it draws its particular strength, Herein, to be sure, one finds an echo of the immediate past, a dialogue with the victimized and the message of an inspiring people who perished under desparate conditions but bequeathed no lasting despair. Dr. Viktor Frankl's observations are, therefore, an invaluable source testifying to this truth.

Yet, there is reserved a special place for the writer and poet who were distant witnesses to the *Shoah,* and whose contribution is essential in order to perpetuate the internal picture of the exterminated part of European Jewry whom they personally and intimately knew as a living, creative and vibrant community. We refer to those who considered it their sacred task to write about and describe those Jewish communities whence they came and whose traditions, character and Jewish pride they remembered and personally inherited. They indeed have a special duty to immortalize and mourn a life which was so cruelly extinguished.

The unfortunate victims of the Ghetto, camps, partisans and hide-outs, who perished or survived have written and write respectively from the point of view of mourners and chroniclers of terrifying events. These writers lack obvious perspective. The mourners or victims have no perspective nor any objectivity. They are withdrawn into their own little subjective world of protest, accusation, righteous indignation, and continuous sorrow and bereavement. The direct witnesses struggle with the aspects of the past terror and with the prospects of what could have been had the world come to our aid. Therefore, from an objective historical point of view, exactly those who were outside the exterminaton scene have much greater ability to assess objectively the overall loss and the enormity of our national tragedy. We ought greatly to appreciate particularly those poets who attempted and succeeded in perpetuating a living recollection of our murdered people and who keep reminding us of our enormous loss.

When I lament you, my birthplace
I mourn my own destruction in yours.
I visualize my childhood and youth from afar,
As they once were and no more . . .
I see my home as if it's still standing there
And alive —
And from the distance,
I long so much for them . . .
I reach out to them and hold on
As if in an inextricable bond.
I will not age even in my old age,
For my strength I derive from that source . . .
Oh my childhood and youth
In your Churban they were destroyed,
With the annihilation of my people,
My past was lost forever.

Suddenly, I became so old,
An old worn out man,
Who stretches out upon the heaps of your destruction —
Who carries his elegy —
And in his eyes that dimmed,
There are no more tears . . .

— Efraim Lisitzki, "L'Ir Moladeti"

This preface to Ephraim Lisitzki's poem is the essential summary of the lament for those communities that once were and will never arise again. Any further comment would be superfluous:

My birthplace, the world of my past,
My hometown . . . you went up in smoke.
. . . Your day is gone . . .
The enemy descended upon your blood
To destroy an eternal people.

My people were led there to the slaughter —
You are not only a past.
You became but a memory.
You became a grave yard
Of my people's sacred victims.
The tombstone of the world of my past,
Even the skies over you
Have bent down in silence.

— Sh. Shtein, "Ayarat Bat Oni"

The old home is no longer only one's birthplace, but the graveyard of Jewish life, the tombstone of a living Jewish community, and that memory is all that remains.

There's no longer a hamlet
In the countries of the North.
Lost and destroyed . . .
Only a memory is left of the hamlet
Haunting the soul
Day and night.

— Yaakov Davdon, "Ayarah Li K'tanah"

This following excerpt is an additional example of the sort of poetry which was written by one not himself a victim. It is, in fact, traumatically more alarming and more urgent in its impact.

> How can I pray — while around me, each time
> I want to sing —
> I see visions of extermination:
> Brothers slaughtered like sheep,
> Brothers lost forever.
> How I wish I could learn to be silent,
> Hold my tears and choke my cries —
> Silence in face of calamity
> Is much more exalting.
> Woe unto me, I do not know how to be silent! . . .
> Accursed be exulation!
> Damned be beauty!
> Shoah! Shoah! Shoah!
>
> — Shin Shalom, "Shoah"

How can one deal with any *Shoah* theme and not encounter the theme of despair? No matter what one reads, despair will naturally percolate through. The Ghetto writer confronted this very painful truth. His counterpart outside the Ghetto scene stood shocked, bereft, confused, frightened and helpless. He could only eulogize the *Churban* of his people, or be silent:

> Alas, how I wish I could learn to be silent.
>
> — Ibid

Or to the contrary:

> No, I will not carry the terror in silence.
> Like the birds will I shriek bitterly
> Mourning and moaning.
>
> — Mordechai Temkin, "B'tzel Beyti Echese"

There is also the case of the poet who, in despair, escapes into solitude:

> Extinguish yourself my bright world.

Turn to the weeping oak.
Don't let me realize what's happening
Or be able to predict.
No, let my brother hear no more,
The song of my slaughtered heart . . .

— Shin Shalom, "Kveh Olami Habahir"

Or perhaps the poet bursts out in a bitter cry, claps his hands and proclaims:

Tear apart the heavens
And let the stars descend
To mourn . . .
The day has come
When man has lamented
On the strings of his flesh
From the depths of his blood
That gushes like a faucet.
And he raises his tongue
In broad daylight like a flag,
Like a marker at the crossroads.
For the depths have covered
The word of the heart and mouth,
And no ear on earth
Will listen to his speech —
Who needs to hearken to
Sophisticated talk?

And prayer and pain
Despair and vision
Ascend in the sanguine sunrise.
And if you were to beat your head against the wall,
Before the world,
From delirium of pain,
And you were to tear out your hair
From the bitterness of annihilation
To weave a rope
To bind the dispersed —
Will a heart somewhere tremble?

When O When? Who may know
When will the day of revenge arrive

For the lives that were destroyed
And reduced to dust and ashes?

Is there yet a day to be found in time of retribution
Before eyes dim from crying
And their world is darkened forever?

— Shachna Neshkes, "Kiru Hashamaim"

Thus, the despair theme in the poetry-of-despair reflects the feelings of the individual Jew while tortured or dying on the gallows as much as the collective perception of the reality of its daily bitter lot.

There is no doubt that the spark of hope never faded from the people whether in the Ghettos or even the camps. Their hope flickered until the last moments that someone would survive and tell the world what had really happened. One thing we shall never know or dare to second guess is the last thought of the perishing in the gas chambers when the ultimate reality of their death was revealed. The martyrs hoped against hope for some sort of miracle, but it never occured. On their way to death, they knew that death had come.

In the last verse of Yitzchak Katzenelson's epic written January 15-17, 1944, he summarizes our people's tragedy, its spiritual and psychological-crisis and its historic meaning, and perhaps it ought to serve as a warning, instruction, or consitute the martyrs' last desperate thoughts in face of their death.

Woe unto me, all has ended —
There was a nation and it is no more,
There was a people and no longer —
It is all over!
It's like a story —
The beginning is found in our Torah —
And up till today —
A sad story yet who says that's beautiful?
A story about the Amalekite and one more evil
Than he —
The German . . .
O far away heavens,
O wide earth,
O great seas —
Do not roll up into a ball
To destroy the evildoers from the surface of the

Earth
Let them destroy themselves!

— "The Song of the Slaughtered Jewish People"

And perhaps in an ancient Midrash a pointed interpretation has been found that fathoms the depth of the Shoah which defies any understanding.

> Said Elijah to Moses: an edict has been
> issued from above to annihilate your children. Moses replied: If the decree has been sealed in clay, my prayers will be heard. And if in blood — what has been decreed cannot be reversed.
>
> — *Midrash Esther*

NOTES

1. *Bletter Far Geshichte,* Yivo, April-July, 1948.
2. *Bletter Far Geshichte,* Yivo, Vol. 1, p. 104, 1948.
3. *Judenrat,* Dr. Isaiah Trunk, N.Y.C. The MacMillan Company, 1972.
4. *The Clock Above the Head,* A. Datzetnik, p. 29, "Now to die is no heroism. Now to live is."

IV

THE WORLD STANDS ACCUSED

All my roots were torn out
Where can I reroot them again,
The voice of my blood cries
From the gloom of every wound.
The cloud weeps:
The whole world is guilty!
My lament dissipates without an echo
In the night of murder.
Cain extinguishes the stars in the sky.

— B. Mordechai, "Balaylah"

One of the most remarkable and depressing aspects of the Holocaust era was the fact that so many members of the educated strata did not lift a finger to prevent the Nazi slaughter of the Jews. (As a matter of record most of the *Einsatzkommandos* had college degrees and many among them had Ph.D's in divinity, medicine, jurisprudence and in philosophy.) Well known humanitarians, spiritual leaders, literati, and philosophers seemed to have joined in a collusion of silent indifference to the human targets of Nazi annihilation.

The poet Shin Shalom asks:

. . . Why the silence?
Why do you stand aloof?
Why are you mute
Ye shephards of idols?
Don't you perceive,
That together

With my people,
Abandoned for destruction,
Your own future is murdered
And devastated to the ground?
How dare you ignore it forever? . . .

— "Azakah"

It is possible then to safely assume that the *Shoah* tragedy was a result of humanity's moral and ethical collapse, shown by its collective indifference and cruel silence. Humane sensitivity disappeared. It lost its nerve to protest against cruelty and its courage to resist unfathomed evil. It appeared that Western culture, which derived its vitality from Christianity, had shallow roots of moral commitment. Its followers demonstrated an amazing ability and aptitude to adjust to the Nazi regime and tolerate Nazi ideology. If they were not directly supportive, they certainly consented by their silence. How else can it be explained that an entire society became overnight the receptacle of racial theories of hate, and its conveyor of mass murder?

Yaakov Fichman concluded, therefore, that those "Dark Powers" within the people were actively functioning during the deceiving evolution of human and social progress during the century preceding the *Shoah*. The "Black Forest" that sprang up and rapidly spread in the nooks and crannies of society, actually undermined the foundations of humanity's morality, until the "eternal pillars shuddered and fell."[1] Germany thus exposed and demonstrated "all the defilement within her" and became the embodiment of Europe's evil. For this reason and this reason alone, Germany will never be able to whitewash this immoral stain from her national physiognomy:

The immeasurable abyss which you have unveiled
Your obscene reputation will haunt
generations
which will be horrified recalling your darkness.

— "L'uma Zo"

Zalman Shneur saw this Nazi monster from a psychological and historical perspective, or perhaps more exactly, from the aspect of the Devil's dialectic. He perceived the world as incapable of advancing along the path of spiritual and moral progress. On the contrary: "The old wheel is grinding on its axle with a rusty old screech." This is to say, that history moves deviously backward. Thus Shneur returns again and again to the same theme of Europe's shaky spiritual foundation which lacks uncompromising morality:

. . . She threw off her priestly mantle
And bedecked herself with colored flags.
She has a deceiving smile
And eye-shadow on her lids.
Her hairdo is that of a prostitute before sunset.
Under her robe embroidered with eagles and regal scepters
Wicked fists are clenching
And weapons of destruction open their mouths . . .

— "Y'mey Habeynayim Mitkarvim"

Abraham Shlonsky represented the politically progressive socialist wing in Hebrew poetry. In great disappointment he unleashed his bitter anger at the blindness of the nations whom he had once trusted, and accused them for not coming to the aid of his people in its agonizing plight and of neglecting to take seriously the signs of the oncoming storm which "warned them with thunderbolts," but, "they were too obtuse, their eyes were bleary." In his poem: "Ask the Burnt in Fire" he inquires:

Has the Kingdom of Darkness returned?
Have the Middle Ages made a comeback?
Or perhaps Attila has returned to reign again,
And by the prowess of his arm to subjugate once more?
Who ever thought that in our time,
Hands would be found to ignite the hellish fires
Of the Auto Da-Fe pyres?

— "Sha'alu S'rufim Ba'esh"

Shlonsky's conclusion coincides with that of Fichman's. Both maintain that forgiveness is impossible for mankind's perfidious behavior in the face of our people's destruction. Upon us, says Shlonsky, rests the sacred duty to remember not to forget:

By these eyes that have seen the woe and grief,
Their outcries heaving to my heart's embrace,
By compassion which taught me to condone and forsake
Till days have come too awful for grace
I have taken this oath as I breathe and live:
To remember everything, every place
To remember — and not a thing forget . . .

— "Neder"

No less powerful are the memorable words of Yitzchak Lamdan which read like an oath to keep the *Shoah* indelibly imprinted upon the memory of every Jew and every decent human being:

In the name of the Holocaust
For which there are not enough tears to bewail,
Nor a cry profound enough to contain its sadness
And the bitterest eulogy is muted confronting it.
I therefore surrender my days
To a memory of anger
And deny myself the pleasure of oblivion.

— "B'shem"

As for Hitler's partners in crime, his Nazi hordes and their Nazi fellow travellers from all over Europe and elsewhere, they will stand condemned for direct conspiracy in the annals of moral history. About the pious pretenders and hypocrites Chaya Vered had this to say:

This was a world that hid in newspapers,
And melted in tears of mercy,
While the sheep was trampled in its blood . . .

— "Al Cherev Umeytar"

And Ephraim Lisitzky laments:

Your shame you don't cover
Even with a fig leaf,
Your nakedness you expose

Without shame or embarrassment,
You world reformers and the planners
Of its future . . .
Why do you so cunningly disguise yourselves
With worthless masks that embellish deceit
Which cover up all seven abominations
In your hearts . . .?
With glorious pride
You raise your wicked fist,
In lies, malice and flattery
You praise yourselves
And boast within the gates.
And upon the judgment seat
You enthrone yourselves
To mete out verdicts
Over the lackeys of a world destroyer —
Surely him you ought to thank.
Public reprimand is in your throat
Private praise you hide in your heart.
He teaches you the art of governing
For he will legislate for you ancient laws
Of the jungle, upon which you will base
The world and everything within it.
What he has done against you,
You have already forgiven him.
For his bloodshed you pardoned him
And reconciled yourselves to your own ruins,
Which he caused you with his own hands.

— "B'efes Aley T'eynah"

The irony of it all is that those sentences meted out against the Nazis proved too lenient to be of any didactic import despite the enormous evidence of their crimes. The attempt to pardon all Nazi war criminals thirty five years after the war is telling. The imperative lesson that every living Nazi guilty of war crimes is subject to prosecution as long as he lives, has lost its impetus in a world that wishes to forget and forgive . . .

Thus, the obvious anguish of the poets who have been confronted with this stark reality of moral deceit and moral compromise in the world they live in:

Alas, how did this world turn into a Sodom?

Alas, how could this world watch our blood gushing?
Alas, how were we abandoned by God and men?
Alas, why were we murdered in view of the
whole world for no sin at all?

— Moshe Tabenkin, "Eicha-Nisa"

Indeed, there was no sin to justify our slaughter. Traditional theodicy was totally rejected. Uri Tzi Greenberg went on the offensive:

> Let's assume we have sinned. So what? Our sin wasn't any greater than that of other nations."

"Rechovot Hanahar"

There is no need for any *apologia pro publico*. There need be no explanations of some imponderable causes that might have been the fantastic reason for our merciless slaughter. The cataclysm that befell us was the consequence of an existing world that is by its very nature:

Such a contemptible world,
Such an abhorrent world,
A world that stood silent
When a fettered people was bleeding to death
A world of murder, evil, lie and deceit.

— David Shimoni, *Sefer Ha-Idilyot*

Despairing of this world has far reaching implications. Our hope was dashed to the ground and trampled by man's bestiality. Our world of positive thinking, of spiritual existentialism, of hope and love, of vision and messianism was gone with the smoke of the crematoria. It is a sad thought.

But I, . . .
Whom shall I love?
I, dazed by the toxic wine of death . . .
All deceived me.
There was none, not even one
In all Sodom, not one exception
Who did not betray me . . .

— Avraham Shlonsky, "Mul Yom Ha'achzavot"

And the poet continues his condemnation:

Forsaken, betrayed and impotent
Woe, vox populi, vox dei,
Both have stunned and disillusioned me . . .

— Ibid

The dissappointment in man is not as much in the awareness that man can turn into a beast, but rather it is the exasperation over man's hypocrisy, his pretense of being compassionate and benvolent. The empty slogans couched in soothing phrasiology were deceptive. The hollow altruism, the proclamations of man's rights to freedom of choice rooted in the spirit of emancipation proved false. For when the critical confrontation was forced upon man, he unveiled how treacherous he could be.

They shut their heart
To the cry of the bereaved,
A false society
Whose lips drip with sweetness
And their haughtiness overwhelms
Everything else . . .

— Binyamin Tene, *B'cheret D'vay*

There are those who contend that it is rationally untenable to accuse the entire world of complicity in guilt by commission or omission in the Holocaust crime. There is reason to differentiate between those who directly participated in the excesses of the *Shoah,* and those who have knowingly or unknowingly reacted the way they thought best for their own self protection, and in some way adjusted to life in the then existent situation.

Ephraim Lisitzky challenges this viewpoint. In his rebuttal he offers a scathing accusation, particularly at the end of his famous poem: "Hitler Before the Seat of Judgment".

In this poem, Hitler is described as being on trial for his crimes. After the accusing statement against him, Hitler rises in his own defense and offers a denial that he alone bears responsibility for the Holocaust. He summarily includes as his partners in crime the entire German nation and all the enlightened nations who helped him in a variety of ways to execute to the fullest his bloody Final Solution. Thus he concludes:

> . . . Your verdict,
> I don't know, but before you pronounce it . . .
> Let it be known, honorable judges
> That my spirit you will not eradicate.
> It dwells within their spirit,
> For this is their true spirit!
> They wear masks of righteousness,
> Kindness and compassion —
> With Christian charity
> They mask their spirit . . .
>
> If they stuff their ears not to hear the truth
> I will laugh and mock them . . .
> My scorn I will make them hear
> From the top of my gallow . . .
> From the slope of my scaffold
> Will I shout:
> "Assembly of liars that you are,
> Sycophants, hypocrites,
> Two-faced pious prostitutes"!
>
> — E. Lisitzky, "Hitler Before the Seat of Judgment"

The anger of the Jews and their poets was painful. Some of the reasons have been repeatedly considered. One additonal aspect ought to be mentioned regarding the premeditated conspiracy against the Jews. The excuse given for not making the extermination of European Jewry a political and international issue, was that the Nazi atrocities were in the category of "Internal Affairs". It was the Roosevelt Administration and the British Government that led the macabre parade in white gloves which closed the doors to North and South America, to England and to Palestine, preventing the rescue of as many Jews as possible from a certain death.[2]

Indeed, many could have been rescued in a variety of ways. It is too heartrending to recall the tragic affair of the ship "St. Louis" with its cargo of over nine hundred Jewish people. It is, however, noteworthy to recall a not too well known fact, in regard to the "St. Louis" affair.

When Cuba, which originally granted entry visas, refused to allow the nine hundred and seven Jews to disembark, Cardinal Mundelein of Chicago, and the then President of the C.I.O., John L. Lewis, endeavored to persuade President Roosevelt to allow entry of the refugees to the United States but to no avail.[3] The U.S. Government showed no understanding nor compassion. The facts of the Jews' fate in Europe were already well known. In an article published November 24, 1938, in the Nazi newspaper, *Das Schwartze Korps,* the policy was clearly enunciated: with the outbreak of the forthcoming war the Jews of Europe were scheduled to be liquidated.

In view of this awareness, does one wonder why the bitterness against the free world was so profound and irreconcilable in the hearts of the doomed and their poets? To compound the aforementioned callousness towards the 907 victims at the shores of America, we ought to recall still a greater tragedy directly abetted by the Turks and the British on the Black Sea. The ship was named "Struma"; its cargo, 769 Jewish escapees from under the Nazi sword, fleeing from the shores of Rumania. Its destination: Palestine.[4]

The British gentlemen in cooperation with Turkish authorities indirectly conspired against the refugees. England lived by the dictates of the notorious "White Paper." In short, they enabled (it is suspected) the German submarine to sink the "Struma." The year was February 1942 at the height of Nazi extermination of the Jews of Europe.[5]

The poet Michael Deshe immortalizes the "Struma" disaster in the following verses:

> The ship was blown to smithereens,
> The deep swallowed the mass of people,
> The dying have ceased to groan
> The wanderers have found their abode.
> And yet, the world's foundations did not shake
> Nor did the world shudder at the sight.
> Countless are Israel's tears!
> Who is so heroic to carry this burden
> And not tire . . .?!
>
> — Michael Deshe, "S'finat Hayagon"

As to Britian's behavior toward the Jewish plight during those years of terror and extermination, its name will be remembered in the records of the Holocaust story with disdain and abhorrence.

Yaakov Fichman lamented thus:

Woe, the world its doors
Has bolted,
For the escapees from death
No nation rose to open its doors
Abomination deformed the face of the world.

— 'B'chi Yameynu"

The pervasive absence of moral and humane responsibility demonstrated itself all over in the form of aberrant callousness. Even the deceptively peaceful Switzerland proved to be as guilty in its quiet conspiracy against the Jews by its attitude toward the rescue of the victims of Nazism.

Chaim Guri wrote with scorching sarcasm upon his visit there in 1947:

The evident calm is suspect

For after all . . .
My blood was never spilled here.

— "Pirchey Esh"

Verily on the threshold of Switzerland lies her sin . . . Switzerland was centrally located in Europe. Switzerland could have become a blessed escape route for many Jews who perished at the hand of the Nazis. Switzerland was reluctant and uncooperative in rescuing Jews.[6]

Serene, an innocent dove you seem.
But not far from your borders
Black smoke rose from crematoria
And hunger held sway.

— Ibid

We should also recall the circulation of the Nazi resurrected "Madagascar Plan" as a ploy to divert attention from the "Final Solution". This anti-Semitic plan was entertained by some European governments before World War Two. France and particularly

Poland were active participants in this seemingly civilized yet treacherous solution of the Jewish problem in Europe. Eventually it lost its impetus but the Nazis revived it, and kept it alive until 1941, to confuse and deceive their Jewish victims.[7]

Israel Efros called this plan "A Cunning Stratagem":

> To open for us with a generous hand
> A distant arid wilderness,
> But not the gates of one certain land . . .

In a further satire on the Madagascar issue permeated with grief, the poet Efros continues to address the nations of the world known to be parading their humanitarianism (like France, Poland, etc.) who covertly wished to rid themselves of their Jews:

> Woe, after thousands of years
> Of the world's love-pangs and worry
> For the fate of our Jewish soul,
> The world has finally taken off its mask
> And unveiled its true face
> Which congeals the blood in our veins
> And petrifies the heart.
> Alas, after a long search and groping for
> generations
> The world opened its eyes
> And shed its cataracts:
> Go Jews, go!
> Join the monkeys and cannibals.
> Return to the wilderness
> Your body and soul.
> How beautiful will be the end
> Of a people that bore the light unto the
> nations.

— "Tachbulat Orma Hi"

Efros continues to reflect upon the world's betrayal of the Jews from the spiritual standpoint and confronts the issue in all its severity.

He portrays "Ecco Homo" nailed on the Cross "without a wreath on His head" castigating and chastising His supposed faithful: "Your silence is a deeper pain, than the most bitter cup of potion" and the poet continues to ask: "Why isn't there an eye to see, nor an ear in the world to hear Israel's anguished cry?" With biting sarcasm he offers his own answer: "Indeed the nations' piety is sheer deceit. They actually imagine that their Saviour is truly dead. He no longer lays a claim on them. There is neither truth nor ethics. but when He, in spite of them, chances into their homes or backyards, their astonishment shocks them at His appearance":

> . . . What? Is He still alive?
> A curse on the head of the hangman
> Who has not finished his job!
> Every shameless maid
> Welcomes me with a pot of scalding water,
> And every dog on the garbage heap
> Smells a savouring scent in my wounds,
> And every door, wicket and crack are shut for me
> Lest I stealthily enter
> And soil their rugs with my blood.
>
> — "Lo Tziparney Ha'ofot Hatmeyim"

Consequently, there is no such thing as a guilty conscience. Evil, wrongdoing, crime and perversion of moral norms are under the circumstances tolerable if not outright acceptable:

> . . . A surging wave of compassion and love,
> To that unfortuante nation,
> That unintentionally deviated from the path.
> An innocent maiden birthed a bastard
> At no fault of hers . . .
>
> — Ibid

After all the family of nations is united by a common bond of attitude, philosophy and value concepts. For this reason one ought not overreact when facing a recalcitrant member nation who has deviated from normative behavior. Blessed thus be the lenient judgement of him, and praised be the forgiver. Isn't this the case in the world today? Has not this been the attitude towards the still living mass murderers in Germany? Have not Austria, South America, Spain and Portugal been havens for Nazi criminals? Has not the United States been silent about the fact that ex-Nazis and Nazi-collaborators have under false pretense entered this country and when apprehended enjoyed the full measure of legal protection?

In view of this appalling attitude, the slaughter of our children becomes the more exacerbatingly acute. The poet Natan Alterman addresses his elegies to the tragedy of the one million murdered Jewish children . . . His accusation is beyond any challenge. A heartless mankind stood witnessing the slaughter of the most innocent of all — our children.

When our children wept
In the shadow of the gallows
We did not hear
The world's outrage.

When our bright Jewish children,
Marched toward the scaffold,
They knew
That
Their blood
Was of no consequence . . .
Their only plea was:
Mother, please don't look!

The world worried about
The safety of paintings and sculptures:
Lest the art treasures be demolished!
But
The art treasures of children's brains
Were crushed on walls
And on the sides of the roads . . .

— "Mikol Ha'amim"

And Shin Shalom bitterly declares:

You stood meekly at a distance
While my brethren were led to their death,
Your mouth you sealed from protesting
At the time when they were served the
guillotine . . .

— "Din"

Samuel Avivi denounces the world for burying the truth, justice and judgment, thus granting "license" to atrocities and terror:

The world is bleeding at its foundations
Your ears are deaf to a mother's cry
In your bosom man's name is desecrated . . .
In a common grave you buried:
Truth, justice and judgment
And between them . . .
You squeezed in an unknown dead child . . .

— "Adamah"

Dostoyevsky once observed: "There is no power in the universe capable of wiping away a child's tear." The greatest Hebrew national poet of this century, Chaim Nachman Bialik, proclaimed:

Cursed be he who demands revenge,
For the blood of a small child.
For Satan has not yet
Created such vengeance . . .

— "Al Hashchitah"

Can our pain be adequately expressed or our anguish truly understood in regard to the murder of our innocent children? Natan Alterman put it this way:

About the suffering of adults
In those days of extermination
Much has been told and known.
But only the heavens do know for sure
The fate that befell our children.

— "Mishpat Hageulah"

About the children in the Ghettos writes Menachem Volfovsky:

Pale children,
Jewish chlidren
In the Ghettos,
Voices lost from weeping and tears,

And the heart disintegrates
From desperate crying:
Where is my mother?
Where are you father?
Nobody answers, nobody knows!
My little brothers and sisters,
Tortured and pained
Born in the darkness of travail, . . .
Terror and horror has covered you . . .
From one end of the land to the other
Trains are carrying emaciated children . . .
Day and night . . .
Like innocent doves
They are slaughtered in the Ghettos.
O God, thou awesome Lord . . .!

— "Yeladim Ivrim Beghetto," *Prager Anthology*

Yes, we have an argument with the world . . . "Where were you when our babies and orphans needed you?" ("Shir Mizmor L'Sheerit Israel," Yaakov Cahan):

I have reconciled myself already
To my people's calamity.
But my people's children's demise
I am unable to accept.

— "Moreh"

Thus writes Itzchak Shalev. There is no reconciliation with the fact of their murder. Our children could have been saved in the tens of thousands. The poetress, Enda Finkerfeld Amir captured the tragedy of our loss in her eulogy addressing the world:

I am a bereft Jewish mother.
I come to you world
With a simple matter:
To ask you about
Your children's welfare . . .
No matter how old they may be
Don't be frightened of me,
I won't curse them — not me!

I wish them well
To grow up sane and happily . . .

But you world (remember?)
Stood there as a bystander
And witness
And saw the death of my children
Without a sign of distress . . .

You saw, indeed, and witnessed
Without a tremble of madness . . .
Curse your children, I won't ever,
O you complacent world
Because
I was
A mother . . .!

— "Eym Shakulah"

Frankly to reciprocate with hate for the world's indifference and inhumanity to us is futile. Actually there has not yet been conceived an appropriate universal retribution to fit the dimensions and scope of the crimes committed against our people and all other millions who faced a similar fate.

Who will take revenge?
And if revenge is taken
Will it ever restore glory
To man's image?

— Y.L. Bialer, "Biy'kod Pitzi"

Indeed, the divine in man's image seems to have been lost. In that dark but challenging period in man's history, his humanity faded into nothingness and emptied man of his moral content and sensitivity. It will take much effort before man will be able to redeem himself from this moral corruption which he brought upon himself. This, of course, is the sombre contention of the pessimist, and it is disturbing. Unfortunately, this particular indictment against man cannot be successfully rejected in view of man's attitude and behavior patterns during and after the Holocaust apocalypse. The Holocaust has wrought havoc in its wake, and its results are already proving to be devastating and far reaching. It has effected a dehumanizing, desensitizing and demoralizing universal trend. It has proven to have conditioned man to consciously and subconsciously tolerate murder under various guises and excuses. It rendered man incapable of honest protest against injustice. Everything is measured on a scale of values relative to given conditions and situations. Man's ethical concepts and ideas have been stripped of any absolute values by the new social contract in the post-Holocaust era. In short, the Holocaust debased man and defiled him.

The humanist *qua* optimist, on the other hand, is persistently seeking out signs, even if only a flickering glimmer, of some sort of moral improvement and laying claim to man's inherent redeemability. After all, man has the inalienable right to regret his culpability, and has the ethical and religious claim to expiate his trangressions and crimes, especially when he does it by way of admission and/or confession.

What direction should then man take after having accepted responsibility for the crimes during the Nazi regime? Should admission of guilt be understood as an ethical rehumanization, rehabilitation and restoration of morality, or should we suspect that man's premeditated criminal culpability cannot be atoned for by breast-beating, and that demonstrative *mea culpa* is merely a ruse, a calculated hypocritical piety, meant to divert attention from the roaming culprits?

The poet Yaakov Cohen had already struggled with that very issue in 1941:

> Indeed, this seems to be the lingering pain,
> And the worry becomes more cumbersome
> With the darkness of the nights:
> Will the miracle occur,
> And will man's heart be purified
> In the smelting fires of destruction?
> Will his sight be enlightened by the tragedy
> Will he learn from the torture of the weak
> To help the downtrodden
> The depths of suffering by the smallest of
> Nations
> Evil's prime sacrifice
> And call upon him and proclaim:
> You are my brother!

How could we have tolerated
The burden of your poverty and homelessness
And not have protested the iniquity
Perpetrated against you ever since . . .
Will the miracle of a change for the good
Ever occur?

— "Achen Zeh Hake'ev"

Elsewhere the poet answers his own throbbing questions:

. . . The nations did not awaken . . .
They did not arise to the occasion
To break the oppressor's yoke,
To uproot evil
Proclaim liberty unto all peoples
And build a new world . . .
A world of justice, and peace.
Instead, like cut-throat dealers
Whose eyes are trained on profits
They rush to trade the sacrifice
And enrich themselves from it . . .
Calmly comforting themselves:
Evil, has not yet befallen them . . .

— "Re'u Et Haresha"

This is how the game of life is played out on the immoral trading exchanges of man's market places. Life, morality, welfare, human dignity are traded frequently by the myopic profiteers for ephemeral security. There are no suprises here.

The Nazi atrocities were broadcast to the nations long before their organized application, and were treated phlegmatically. And as to their implicit threat to the Jewish people, they were treated with benign neglect or perhaps stealthily welcomed . . . To this we ought to repeat after the poet with a heart full of disdain:

The nations' sin — the deception of man
World leaders — you set the example.
Your hardened heart — in the dimness of
betrayal
Filled your image with shame,

For you were trapped in your own perfidy.
You failed to sever the wicked arm,
Cunningly you kept yourselves silent
All the while the rivers were filled with
my blood.

— Y.L. Bialer, "Biykod Pitzi"

It takes no great effort to cast aspersions upon an unscrupulous and villainous world. It is not difficult to declare the entire community of man guilty, and expose man's character as appallingly weak, cowardly and venal. But what ought the surviving witness of Auschwitz do when he tries subjectively to assess his life vis-a-vis the world he is inextricably bound to as a human being and a social animal in need of man and society?

How great then is the poet's anguish when he sees that little has really changed. The world of man continues in its decay, and life makes no sense except to live by the instinct of survival. Hence the only alternative left to relieve one's frustration is to bemoan and eulogize the destruction of a world that was meant to give meaning to life and man.

I weep for the demolished world,
For man's voice that was muted . . .

The world is being drained of its blood
. . . Only the moan of the afflicted is heard
As if it were the last gasping sigh . . .
There is no world nor man.
Only ghosts walk in fear,

Who will summon the world to mourn,
To eulogize and bewail?
The flickering lights on world's ruins
Are slowly fading.
The cities are desolate,
The houses are destroyed.
There is no day or sun,
No light nor redemption . . .
I weep over the world's desolation . . .

— Yaakov Rimon, "Ani Boche Al Churban Haolam"

Naturally, there have been reactions of various degrees to the Holocaust cataclysm. The common denominator has been established: The Holocaust is an epochal disaster without historical precedence. This human tragedy has no comparison in the annals of man in its harrowing intensity.

The persistent argument as to what ought to be the most beneficial approach regarding the world's guilt remains unresolved. The fact that an accusing voice reverberates in society, implies the belief that the world has perhaps preserved a degree of sensitivity and justice and that punishment is a catharsis, a road to spiritual rehabilitation of man and that man is after all redeemable. Otherwise there would not have been any value or meaning to any study and serious discussion about the Holocaust.

The poet David Shimoni refuses however to speculate. He summarizes his feelings in cogent terms. He does not hesitate to point at the culprit as he sees it.

> Tell it in Gath and proclaim it
> In the streets of Ashkelon;
> Perchance the Philistines will be frightened,
> And the hearts of the uncircumcised will tremble.
> If we were the only ones to suffer pain,
> Let them then carry the stigma of shame.
> They who stood idly by when . . .
> Our blood flowed like rushing rivers . . .
> On that day of my annihilation
> You Philistines ignored my situation.
> You did not rebel or complain!
> What will you then have to say
> When retribution will come one day,
> When my silent congealed blood
> Will accusingly roar all the way . . .?

— "Hagidu B'Gat"

Up until now we focused our attention on "The World" and its place in the Holocaust scheme as it is reflected in the Hebrew verse. We have seen from the representative examples with how much disdain Hebrew poetry, across all its literary levels, looked upon the world. It is obvious that its attitude is not rooted in some sort of capricious malice. It is rooted in the reality of the Holocaust experiences and as a result it appears to speak with justifiable disgust in regard to the hypocritical world of ours.

Since the Holocaust atrocities took place in the heart of Christian Europe, the role of the Christian community in general and of the individual in particular made all the difference between possible life and certain death for the Jews.

In fact, there were some precious few Christians whose names will be hallowed in the pages of Jewish history for risking their lives and in many cases, dying cruel deaths for helping Jews to hide or escape from the Nazis. But the predominant majority remained frankly indifferent if not hostile, enabling Nazis and their collaborators to destroy the Jews most expeditiously and without concern for interference or obstacles.

In short, this notorious individual and collective behavior, it can be strongly argued, helped exterminate European Jewry.

Hebrew poetry gives its verdict. It maintains above all that every person individually is responsible for acts against humanity. Judaism sets ethics above the state or collective will. Man must defend the universal laws of ethics which mean to protect and preserve life. Otherwise, man loses every justification for his own existence. (Exodus XXIII: 1-2)

For the record, when Hitler came to power he kept up officially respectful relationships with the Catholic and Protestant churches. He understood and appreciated their influential power over all the social and political strata of Europe. However, when he began his transition from theoretical anti-Jewish propaganda to the actual application of physical persecution of Jews, signalled by the "Kristalnacht" in the fall of 1938, the church, with some exceptions, maintained a numb silence. In many cases it even gave spiritual support to fascism. To cite only two examples:

> (1) "The unchangeable will of God meets us in the total reality of our life as it is illuminated by God's revelation. It binds everyone . . . to the natural orders to which we are subject such as family, nation, race . . . In this knowledge we thank God the Lord that he has given to our people in its need a leader (Hitler) as a 'pious and faithful sovereign' . . ."[8]
>
> (2) The Catholic Cardinal of Cologne called upon the faithful:
>
> "To whom the voice of the church is holy, to be loyal to the legitimate authority and conscientiously fulfill their civil duties, re-

jecting on principle all illegal or revolutionary non-cooperation." In 1933 the German Catholic Bishops explaining their criticism of the Nazi system, which was made regarding "assaults upon church rights and property", concluded, that their criticism "do not imply any hidden reservations with regard to the new state. Under no circumstances would we seek to deprive the state of the virtues of the church and we may not do so."[9]

The martyred Protestant Minister Dietrich Bonhoeffer, and Pope Pius XI's encyclical of 1937, "Mit Brennender Sorge," and other sensitive and great souls that appeared intermittently, have actually redeemed Christianity from total moral bankruptcy in the face of Nazism and the Holocaust inferno.

Important studies by Christian scholars have already appeared which verify the contention that Christianity across all denominational levels and groups faced moral fiasco and that its morality foundered on the mechanical precision of the Nazi extermination of European Jewry. Deep seated anti-Semitism in the conservative and liberal churches alike contributed to the extermination of Jews. When Hitler's "endloesung" went into high gear, the Jews were left helpless. Not only the Religionists but even the Socialists and Communists never bothered to concern themselves with the murder of Jews. Their inbred Christian anti-Semitism was too integral in their psyche. Karl Marx contributed his share too.[10] The large net of national underground movements that fought the Nazis all over Europe made no known effort to sabotage the transports on their way to the death factories. The scattered heroic efforts of Jewish resistance within the Ghettos and Concentration Camps were virtually intramural self-propelled movements. The outside Christian world stood there and looked on offering no significant support.

One additional painful fact ought to be mentioned. The Eastern European peoples were all under the oppressive Nazi occupation. The Poles among whom three and one half million Jews lived, were no favorites of Hitler. The first to suffer the extermination of its intellectual and aristocratic elite were the Poles. Logically, the Poles should have become our natural allies. But this did not occur. Their inbred pathological anti-Semitism of chronic dimensions was so profoundly and psychologically binding it rendered them impotent to rise and to vindicate their humanity towards their fellow man.[11]

These were, and still are, the products of a conspiracy of the wrong emphasis on religious teachings that would have gladdened the hearts of Justin, Marcion, Origen, Cyprian, Urban II, Thomas De Torquemada and many more church anti-Semites who contributed immensely to the end results of the Nazi war against the Jews. The long story of degrading the Jew by derision and deicide accusations gave much reason for the thriving of a diluted sort of Christianity which provided fertile soil for a festering anti-Semitism. In the nineteenth century a group of anti-Semites grew out of this soil, with religious, psychological, sociological, economic and political theories which readied the stage for the "Final Solution." (Guozo Istocy in Hungary, Edouard Drumont in France, and Eugene Duehring in Germany — among others —)

This pathological anti-Semitism became inseparable from the thought-stance of many people. They were so infested with this hate virus, that, as historian Simon Bernfeld observed, "Even those Christian scholars who maintained that Jesus never existed concur that the Jews crucified him."

Franklin H. Littell's profound scholarly analysis[12] of three levels of anti-Semitism in Christianity which have led to the monstrous destruction of the Holocaust are:

(1) *Theological Anti-Semitism* which is the product of Christian apologetics created by the Gentile church which replaced the original Jewish sect. It is the Christian triumphalism which maintains that God is done with the old Israel and that Judaism has been replaced by the new Israel, the Gentile church in a new convenant. (Thus the name: The New Testament.) This theological anti-Semitism of declaring the Jew inferior to the Christian was defined at the Synod of Evira (305 C.E.) and confirmed at Nicea (325 C.E.). This theological virus infected Christianity and it is still lingering on despite the Vatican II declaration on the issue of deicide.

(2) *Cultural Anti-Semitism* is built upon the theological foundations. Anti-Semitic Jewish character defamings, caricature and emotional provocations were "programmed" into the culture. Throughout the long centuries anti-Semitic innuendoes, words, phrases were injected into the daily vernacular. This "Malaise of Anti-Semitism" became endemic in Christendom: The most primitive forms of utterances can trigger an outburst of virulent bigotry and may spontaneously create mob action to desecrate synagogues, kill Jews and burn their homes.[13]

(3) *Intentional Anti-Semitism,* a pseudonym of political anti-

Semitism "functions as an ideological weapon". Thus for Hitler or Stalin "political anti-Semitism is planned warfare". We are told that Hilter clearly declared to the German bishops that what he was about to do to the Jews was in concert with and in pursuance of the "Fourth Lateran Council of 1215 A.D.". Thus sheer vociferous and slanderous anti-Semitism could not have mounted upon the "Final Solution" were it not for the theological and cultural background underpinning it.[14]

Hebrew poetry contains reflections on these subjects.

Israel Efros, the poet-philosopher, asks pensively:

> Who said: "Man"?
> I am a beast . . .
> The primoridal beast!
>
> — "Anachnu Hador"

Perhaps Efros had in mind Friedrich W. Nietzsche's rejection of the definition of "man" in Judaism as a cultivated being, sensitized by the ethos of the Torah. Nietzsche rejected the Jew with his ethics as well as "Bethlehem" Christianity which he saw as an offshoot of Judaism as too moral, too ethical and too charitable. He looked toward the virile, bestial Teuton to free himself from these fetters. In *Thus Spake Zarathustra* he proclaims the advent of the "superman" the creator of a super race, a race that is governed by its natural instincts, that rules and subjugates, a new race "for the Lords of the Earth."

This primitive and cruel Homo sapiens could be found in Auschwitz whistling a Wagnerian aria while condemning thousands of people to death. Syllogistically speaking:

> (if) Man is part of mankind
> (and) The Nazi criminal is a human being
> Therefore he is part of humanity.

Were we to follow this rationalization to its logical conclusion we could safely say: Yes, the murderers were an inseparable part of the human race of which we too, the victims, are an inextricable part.

B. Mordecai formulated this truth poetically:

> And if I don't have

A sign on my forehead
For the murder of a brother
(Because I am the murdered) —
I am embarrassed and ashamed
For Cain and I
Sucked at the same mother's breast,
And my blood is as red as his,
And my name is the same as his,
"Adam"!

— "Shirat Ha'eden He'avud"

Elisha Rudin reflected:

Weren't it for Hitler,
We would have forgotten
That man possesses within him
Infamy and shame . . .
Woe, unto our offspring whom we raised —
To be destroyed by man's abomination,
To our shame, and disgrace
For he too had a human face!

— "Laben"

This psychological affront gnaws away at us, for how can we admit that our fellow man is capable of turning into a voracious murderer who kills for joy?

Shaul Tschernichovsky put it succinctly:

Man turned into a wild beast
And every man is a wolf.

— "Baladat Haze'ev"

With more sarcasm and desperation Michael Deshe confronts the truth of man's bestiality:

Don't be surprised
Don't condemn man
His cruelty is his game

Don't despise the son of man
Like a child he loves to play in blood.

— "Urim B'lev Yam"

Every person needs an incentive. The Nazis did not need one in their criminality. They enthusiastically welcomed the opportunity to show their Teutonic insensitivity and showed no trace of remorse at the slaughter of humans:

In these days,
The beast from within man
Leaps forward
With fearsome darkness
From hidden caves.
A frightening monster,
Is ready to devour the world.

— Yaakov Rimon, "Belev Hayamim"

It is clear, that the motif of "The Beast in Man" gave tangible meaning to Nazi bestiality, and Hebrew poetry relentlessly pursued this topic. This is how Avigdor Hameiri sums up the essential reality of mankind, and with great disappointment he speaks of the bitter truth:

Human society that roams in confusion
The stammerers will call them: Beasts of prey.
Is there such an animal in existence
Which possesses a rational mind
To tear apart living creatures without devouring
To take pleasure in the suffering
Of other living creatures . . .?

Whoever expected the offshoot of Goethe
To be so monstrous
To put everything to naught
Upon an instant?

A new monster governs the world
Its theory: "Murder without good reason"
Without hope for good . . .

The masses of Satan's servants
A veritable collection of scum
Are entertained at their fete
By man's groaning
When buried alive.

— "B'maarbolet"

Similar to Hameiri's poem, are the following verses by Joseph Patai with an additional emphasis on man's dastardliness:

How have you degraded yourself O man
How have you descended to abysmal depths
You cast heaven's crown from your forehead
You have discarded God's image from your head.

You acted more wickedly than lurking beasts,
You turned an inhabited Earth into a wasteland.
You murdered, burned and closed your ears,
Even your culture is a product of sinful brutes.

Crematoria for man you have erected
Destructive traps in the depth of the abyss
You have ascended to great heights
Where you have become a bird of prey.

— "Eichah Shafalta Adam"

We have not found in any of the preceding verses any particular indication for an answer to the question we implied previously: Is man personally guilty for the criminal acts perpetrated or is he justified to hide behind the silent masses and claim the right of self-preservation?

It should be kept in mind that in the character and spirit of the Nazi trials we find an amazing and disturbing partial answer to our question.

It became evident from the Nuremberg trials and thereafter that the intent of the international court was to establish the guilt of particular culprits, and in no way was there any proclivity to determine the guilt of the masses or the nations as such for their silent conspiracy in the crimes.

We heard many of the criminal's arguments. Their general claim was their obligations to the state and to obey the command of their leaders. They performed a "task" and if murdering innocent people and children was part of it they had to do it whether they liked it or not . . .

In Ephraim Lisitzky's poem, after the defense for Hitler concluded its summation, Hitler is permitted to speak in his own behalf:

> . . . By the nature and proceedings of this trial
> Can one really distinctly establish
> Who is guilty and who is not?
> If I am to be placed in the accused's dock
> My people must join me there.
> Yes, my people who in their myriads
> Supported me whole heartedly . . .
> I did not exterminate people in secret
> I did it in broad daylight, right in the streets
> Where I drew the spurt of the Jew's repulsive
> blood!
>
> . . . And when he was burning,
> In the open pits and crematoria,
> I did it before my people's eyes.
> Their embers were smoking and fuming . . .
> They . . .Saw it . . .
> They smelled it from up close . . .
> Yet, none of them uttered a whisper
> Not a whimper . . .
> They gladly accepted my deed.
>
> I am but their surrogate
> Their obedient servant . . .
> I am my people!
> And my people is me!
>
> — "Hitler Before the Seat of Judgment"

The claim of the Nazis is true in this case. They did not act in secrecy. By the summer of 1941 they acted openly. In many instances they did not even bother to transport the people to any central location. They slaughtered them on the outskirts of towns, or in the nearby forests or ravines. All German forces, in one capacity or another, the entire civilian and military administrations, industry, railroad system — all contributed, each with their particular capacity and authority, directly or indirectly, in this gargantuan mass annihilation of about eleven million people among them six million Jews. There was hardly a German family that did not have one of its members involved in the extermination theatre. The German postal service carried from "Ost," from Eastern Europe, and from the West, packages from fathers and sons, precious goods looted from their Jewish victims. Who dares to accept the German lie that they did not know what was done to the Jews of Europe? On this point all Holocaust students fully agree.[15]

The other question posed was whether the ingrained hatred for the Jews had as its source Christianity's anti-Jewish teachings. The facts have been thoroughly investigated by prominent scholars. There may be various degrees of assessment but none disagree as to the basic premise. It is to the credit of Christian scholars, theologians and historians like Franklin Littell, Roy Eckardt, Arthur C. Cochrane, Gordon Zahn, Michael Ryan, Martin Niemoeller, Heinrich Gruueben, D. Herrmann Maas, and others, that they have the courage to admit the failure of the church in the face of Nazism as well as its insignificant role in combatting Nazi extermination of the Jews. They wonder what sort of moral and ethical grounding did the Christian church provide in its long history that when the Nazi onslaught came, their own congregants turned dedicated Nazis in no time and their sadistic proclivity was right there where the "Sturmtruppen" wanted it to be.

In Richard L. Rubenstein's incisive study of the character of Nazi ideology[16] he flatly rejects the popular theory of historians that Nazism should be deemed as a pagan cult.

Nazism did in fact nurture mystical tendencies. It believed in the apotheosis of its Fuhrer rendering Hitler, for instance, a high-priest who symbolized and personified the principle of "blood and race," and in whom the ultimate revelation of the German race's soul manifested itself.[17]

Yet, despite the fact that Nazism appeared to rebel against conventional Christian religious establishment and manifestly discarded the principles of Christianity's ethical teachings, nevertheless the Nazis considered themselves full fledged members of the church. In addition, Nazism had no qualms nor any hesitations to embrace and gladly adopt the anachronistic aspects of the church's anti-Semitic theories, traditions and myths so prevalent for centuries in Christendom.[18] There was not a Christian theologian or thinker throughout the ages who slurred the Jews whom the Nazis did not incorporate into their propaganda against the Jews. Ergo, from this particular aspect there was nothing innovative in their approach. Their particular contribution was in creating greater impetus to the hatred for the Jews. They created an atmosphere of utmost urgency to resolve the Jewish presence, by the eradication of the Jewish factor from the midst of European culture and society. Thus the Nazis translated the anachronistic anti-Semitic canard into a brutal and fanatical physical liquidation of the Jewish people in every conceivable way without compromise or delay.

In the historical contest between Christianity and Judaism, Christian leaders seemed satisfied if and when they could persuade the Jews to accept Jesus' divinity. In fact a Jewish convert to Christianity was well treated. The Nazis rejected, however, any alternative. As a matter of fact, they considered Jewish converts to Christianity as Jews and treated them as Jews. By the Nazi definition "a Jew, is a Jew, is a Jew" namely, no matter how "Christianized" and baptized" the Jew may have been, in the Nazi definition he was a Jew down to the third generation. In short, the resolution of the "Judenfrage" was conceived by the Nazis as a total irreversible physical elimination of the Jews.[19]

And finally, it must be also noted that the church's moral inadequacy during the Hitler regime was not exclusively because of its endemic *Kulturantisemitismus* but also because of its inherent conscious adaptability to temporal powers. Accordingly, Hebrew poetry did not remain silent on the subject of Christianity's role prior to the Holocaust and during the Holocaust. The Jewish memory saturated with the blood of its murdered people could not help but look upon the church, the Cross and its symbols not as symbols of grace, compassion and love. For in the desperate hour of our annihilation, the church failed to come to our rescue in an act of selfless humane compassion. It had all the calculated pious reasons but the right one:

Only the Cross is kissed,
This blood-partner of yore.
Indeed, it is of iron
From which swords are also made . . .
Yea, kiss the cold symbol gracefully man
And mumble: "Adam, he is human"

But in his heart he is full of beastliness.

— Pinchas Peli, "Al Hadam"

The outspoken poet Uri Tzvi Greenberg has no patience for euphemisms on this subject. He attacks the Teutonic mentality which apparently never left the cave:

The Christian leaders
Are not of my Bethlehem . . .
They come from the forests,
They are still idol worshippers
With pitchfork, axe and spear . . .

— "Rechovot Hanahar"

In fact, Greenberg argues that Christianity and her Christians are a guise:

. . . And outwardly — polite religiosity,
Majestic churches, beautiful celebrations
Splendiferous art, haloed head, wreath
of flowers
And inwardly . . . the Christians follow
The way of Wotan . . .
A wild beast's mentality . . .
A wild beast, a prisoner of civilized laws . . .

— Ibid

Greenberg is aware of the two sorts of Christianity which differ substantially from each other. The one born in Bethlehem, within the ethics of Judaism: sensitive, compassionate, moral and altruistic. And the gentile Christianity, the Aryan and Wotanized Christianity: primitive, ego centered, intolerant and possessive. The present revisionist movement within the church, in view of the Holocaust experience, is in fact an attempt to free Christianity from the corrosive barnacles of its pagan or Wotanized acculturation, and restore the original ethics of its birthplace. It has been acknowledged that because of this historic departure from original Christian thinking and ethics, Christianity internalized that sort of negativism and disdain for the Jew which eventually contributed immensely to the "hate the Jew" syndrome which prepared the masses to psychologically accept, or tolerate the Nazi-led extermination of the Jews.

This Christian primitivism ran deep particularly in the Eastern European areas. In a characteristic ballad, "The Last Jew." Shlomo Skolsky, describes the mood of the disgruntled masses of villagers right after having collaborated with the Nazis in murdering their local Jewish population. Intuitively, they felt that something was not altogether right. They were restless and edgy. They sensed that one more Jew still remained among them. They looked and searched everywhere to no avail. Suddenly, lo and behold, they finally discovered him. Guess where? On the Cross! This was "the last Jew" and of him, too, they had to rid themselves and with a vengeance at that . . .

> The pitchforks were raging
> The axes in their hands were ready
> for engaging
> Here is the Jew! Let's get up and get
> him down
> They climbed upon the Cross up high
> And covered Jesus' statue with their axes'
> might . . .
> You are the Jew, they shouted in anger's
> fright
> Climbing and pushing each other outright.
> Why do they thrash him with so much fierceness
> Grinding their teeth and pitchfork briskness?
> Today is requital time, for all we know
> The wicked a brutal party are having and
> making a row!

In his poem "God and His Gentiles", Uri Tzvi Greenberg describes God as having descended upon the thresholds of the European cathedrals and asking those who enter:

> Where are my Jews who used to live here?
> I don't hear their voices anymore in
> Heaven up there . . .!
> And the gentiles fearlessly replied:
> Germans came here and we joined in collusion
> We killed . . . them all, the young and the old
> We hated them from the days of old

When you came on the Cross, *Pater Noster!*
We thought You too hated them
So we were taught and told by priests,
By fathers and in the books of youth.
You gave us land to possess and power to rule.
The Jews, the skies you didn't give to cover
them.
They are, indeed, unclaimed and despised
They are at best like a doormat . . .
And lo, the German came and said:
Too many Jews among you
Let us destroy them, and behold they are no more,
Pater Noster!
And the Lord again took a look at his Christian
flock
And leaned against the gate and a word He didn't say.
And the geniltes as they gazed at the Lord's face
They were stunned by the view
His was the face of the eternal Jew
Even his eyes were Jewish too.
And the cathedral,
Took on the looks of a Synagogue,
And the Cross at the entrance was no more.
The befuddled Christians broke into a roar
Like wild beasts did they groan:
Did a Jew still remain in our midst?
And the Synagogue still stands in town?
Young fellows quick, bring fire
And gasoline cans for a Jew's pyre . . .!

In the following excerpts from Greenberg we find great thematic similarity with that of Skolsky's "The Last Jew," but the plot differs. Skolsky speaks of a perfidious community. Greenberg portrays a prototype, a familiar character, "Ivan son of Stephan Gospodar" and masterfully exposes his true character. This Ivan lived side by side with the Jews and knew them well. Yet his upbringing and prejuidices consumed him with hatred for his Jewish neighbors. When he finally has the opportunity to eliminate the Jews from his midst, he is uncontrollably elated:

. . . They all were taken
Unto the snow covered field!

Even the infant that hid its face
In its mother's breast . . .
In fear and terror
They dug their own graves
At the German's command.
Because: They were Jews . . .

And I, Ivan, the son of Stephan
Was so glad to see it happen . . .
For this is good and right
They lived long enough in the world . . .

What a pleasure Almighty Lord
No more Jews to behold
At home . . .
No! No more Jews today,
They are finished, in the pit,
Hurray! . . .

I, Ivan, the son of Stephan
Stand now in the Synagogue free
This is me, and all this belongs to me!
We are a month away from Christmas day
Almighty Lord.
Their Shofar is all mine
In your honor
O Lord
I will sound it
Really fine! . . .
TUTUTU-TU-TU . . .

And Greenberg continues his imputation without hesitation:

There is not enough compensation
For our tragedy.
Its measure encompasses the universe
The height of the nations' cultural
distinction
Is our Jewish blood! . . .
And its conscience
Is our cry . . .

These severe accusations are not of poetic license. They are real and break forth with their indictment from the depths of Jewish martyrdom and from the anguishing moan of the unhealing wounds of a thousand years of Jewish life in Europe which enriched and civilized the countries of its sojourn with the sort of quality culture which has no comparison or substitute. It hurts!

Abraham Kariv summarized his pain and protest as plainly and pointedly as he was capable of:

> . . . Is there a chicanery around
> With which you did not deceive God and man?
> Is there yet a cruelty to be found
> That does not permeate you?
>
> Is there a perfidious act left
> For Satan's imagination to beget
> Which man's hand has not yet tried
> And in its deed, been defiled?
>
> Alas, your salvation's instruction
> Were my death and destruction.
> Alas, your religion and its laws
> Were my horror and woes.

Is there then any wonder why the Nazis sang of Jewish blood spurting from every soldier's bayonet? The traditional identification with "Iron and Blood" raised generations to think in such specific categories. Furthermore, the sublimation of the Cross and the Crucified that was intended to promote the ideal of altruism, evidently lost its original lofty meaning. When cataclysmic events, like the Nazi fury, were unleashed, and Christian ethics and ideals were put to the supreme test, they failed miserably . . . These stark facts confirm that the Nazis have not only annihilated Jews, Gypsies and so many millions of decent people, but have also exposed Christianity's tenuous moral influence upon its communicants, and in a sense, crucified Jesus a second time and buried the "Bethlehem" Christian ethos. It is history's verdict that the road to hell is paved with good intentions. History also proved Santayana right. Those who refuse to learn from their past mistakes are bound to repeat them in the future. If Christian history and its experience of primitive hate: the Crusade's blood thirsty Bacchanalian Holy War of pious marauding mendicants in the name of a sacred behest; the sadistic inquisition-terror under the Cross, etc., did not give an impetus, a long time ago, to revise, reassess and make metamorphic root changes in philosophy, and stale theological interpretations and to discard tendentious historical lies that were nurtured and preserved for good use throughout the centuries, what could we have expected when the Nazi onslaught descended upon the Jews?

Iron and blood! . . . That's your real redeemer,
Hidden in your sanctuaries for a long, long time.
Thanksgiving offerings you gladly brought Him
And pious supplications you offered in hymn
On every mountain and hill.

Iron and steel were hardened in your temples
Of spilled blood you joyfully sang.
Father his son taught man to subdue
Of arrows and bows mother sang to her babe.

Violin and harp were smashed,
Sword of spade was made
. . . But the mask of your hypocrisy
Was finally torn off your face . . .

The iron sword still cuts
The flesh of the human race,
And blood to blood cries,
From East to West
And everywhere in space . . .

About the slain of nations
Your marches sing,
And your wine of joy
From human skulls you drink.

Noah Pniel, "Al Pitchei T'hom"

We have seen thus, that the triumvirate of mankind, man and Christianity, demonstrated (each it its own way and difference) its betrayal of the Jewish people in the hour of its most desperate struggle. It has reflected the sad fact that in those tragic days there was no justice, no law and no judgment, no kindness, no concern and no compassion. (The little that there was, will be remembered with deference and gratitude. However, to make it signally momentous, as some try, is to embarrass those who did live up to their humane responsibility, and desecrate the memory of those who were murdered.)

All that there really was during those dark years of the catastrophe was: indifference, sarcasm, hypocrisy, barbarity, crematoria, gas-chambers, gallows, open pits, and rampant mass murder for sheer pleasure. Those who did not participate in the actual slaughter were guilty in their perfidious silence. The countries and governments that were capable of rescuing some or many of us and refused, were guilty in conspiring in our annihilation. Particularly painful is Roosevelt's rejection of direct military intervention to disrupt the extermination operations lest he be accused (by whom?) of dragging the U.S. into a "Jewish War" against Germany. He felt, rather we are told, that the war had to be won for democracy. When it was won, the Jews of Europe were dead — and the allied moral victory over Nazism was a total failure. Little did he or the Allies know (or did they want to know?) what Hitler's real intention was. Imagine what sort of a difference there would have been in winning the war had the moral victory truly been the prime objective. One may safely assume that the entire post-war era, its spirit and the global consequences, would have been quite different. Today we are reaping the fruits of the myopic thinking and moral callousness of those war years. These are the facts, and no matter how many attempts will be made to falsify the horrifying dimensions of Hitler's war against the Jewish people, the historic records attest to the truth.

As we have illustrated, the Hebrew poets intrepidly voiced their desperate protest with words written with the blood of their wounded hearts. They did not mince their words and were little concerned lest they offend someone's feelings. They performed their task for history with dedication. They eternalized the accusation articulately and with courage so that future generations might know what actually happened.

NOTES

1. Yaakov Fichman, "Hein Yedanum," *P'at Hassadeli,* p. 21.

2. The actions of the Danish people will remain exemplary in the annals of ethical and moral responsibility. The workers of Holland, too, will be remembered among "the righteous among the nations", who risked their lives to save Jewish lives. The Swedes, Spaniards and Portuguese were helpful. Switzerland's behavior

deserves nothing but condemnation for its reluctance to help, a classical example of pious hypocrisy. The rest of the world's behavior toward the Jews and their indisposition to join in rescuing Jewish lives is their historical infamy to be remembered.

3. Arthur D. Morse: *While Six Million Died,* the subtitle: "A Chronicle of American Apathy". *The Worcester Globe* wrote of the book: "Morse's well-proven thesis that, but for pusillanimity of Roosevelt and Hull, along with their opposite numbers among the other great and free nations, millions of those who perished might have been saved . . .

> Apathy, callousness and political expediency far outweighed the value of human life. Immediate action was needed, and behold, beautiful verbiage and endless delay were all that came forth.

4. Article by Reuben Einstein, *The Jewish Spectator,* June 1967, pages 8-16.

5. For a brief but detailed account, see: *The Holocaust,* by Nora Levin, pages 581-582.

6. For further insight into the behavior of the Swiss authorities and their persistent policy of non-cooperation and non-rescue, see a well documented book on this subject: *The Lifeboat is Full* by Alfred A. Haesler, (Funk & Wagnalls, 1969).

7. *The Final Solution* by Gerald Reitlinger, pages 76-79, the most authoriative study on this subject.

Parenthetically speaking, there is much to be said regarding the fact that in 1937 France supported by Poland led the discussion around the contrived "Madagascar Plan". It is easy to perceive why Hitler and his partners sensed the spirit of Europe and dared *ab initio* to conceive a plan to dispose of the Jews in the bestial manner they did.

Our Jewish tragedy has become insurmountably staggering with the irrefutable evidence that so many governments in a position to prevent the Nazis from achieving such a clear victory over their defenseless victims, cold-bloodedly refused to help. The free world could have rescued the Jews from annihilation. Just imagine, had the Jews been told: the doors of the free world are open for you . . . get out in whichever way possible . . . we stand ready to welcome you. Imagine if morality had won out over political considerations, the Nazis would have needed its entire army to prevent our escape.

If not all Jews, then a great number would have survived. But this was not the case. The contrary was true. The free world augmented its enforcement of immigration admission policies. President Roosevelt wanted to win the war for Democracy first. Britain refused to revoke its notorious and nefarious "White Paper".

We ought to note the tragic paradox about Eichmann and his group. They did agree in the beginning to let Jews immigrate to Palestine.

8. See Cochrane, Arthur C., *The Church's Confession Under Hitler* (Philadelphia: Westminster Press, 1962), page 12. This was the voice of Protestants, June 11, 1934. See also two brilliant addresses by Professor Franklin H. Littell of Temple University, delivered at the Second Annual Conference on the Church Struggle and the Holocaust, at Wayne State University, March 21, 1971, and "The German Church Struggle and the Plight of the Jew" delivered in Jerusalem, August 18-22, 1977.

9. See Zahn, Gordon C., *German Catholics and Hitler's War* (New York: Sheed & Ward, Inc., 1962). In another reference in the same documentary, Zahn recounts the story of an Austrian Catholic peasant Franz Jagerstatter who was beheaded for refusing to serve the army in what he believed to be an "unjust war". In the instructions he received from his Bishop, he was told that he had "no right" to reach such a conclusion nor was justified in taking such a stand.

10. Karl Marx: *A World Without the Jews;* also Glikson: *The Jewish Complex of Karl Marx.*

11. I was born in Poland, I was there when it all happened. Notwithstanding occasional humanitarian acts of individual Poles who risked their lives to save some Jews, the predominant majority of Poles, Ukrainians, Rumanians, Slovaks, Lithuanians and others helped in many ways to destroy the Jews. Their internalized anti-Semitism and pathological jealously and hatred of Jews caused them to lose their human spark. They waited like vultures to loot Jewish homes no sooner had the last Jew left the premises under Nazi guns.
And if this is not enough, when the few emaciated and physically and emotionally desperate Jews returned to Poland after liberation to look for someone of their families that might have survived, Russian soldiers had to stand guard at the places where they temporarily lodged since with the aid of Polish militia the Poles came and killed them one by one lest they demand the return of the goods left with them before deportation, or point a finger at some of them who gladly and voluntarily collaborated with the Nazis. Yes, Poland is saturated also with Jewish blood of many who miraculously survived Concentration Camps, only to find their death at the hands of Poles. How will the Poles explain the Kielce Massacre of the summer of 1945, or the massacre of eight young survivors in Raciaz near Plock? I buried the murdered with my own hands! These are only two cases of many, many more . . . This was the prevailing ethos of the well known "pious" Poles and others.

12. See Littell's monumental study on the failure of Christians to understand the Jewish experience titled: *The Crucifixion of the Jews* (New York: Harper & Row, 1975)

13. History has proven that this was a truism. In recent years of Russian anti-Semitism one may recall the reappearance of several anti-Semitic books of Jewish caricatures by Kichko such as *Judaism Without Embellishment* or the reappearance of the infamous and slanderous book *The Protocols of the Elders of Zion.*

14. And if one may wonder wherefrom comes the genocidal thought, one may point to the writings of the church leader Cyprian (d. 258) who "declared that the peoplehood of the Jews has been cancelled and that Jews can only share the messianic age by conversion and baptism into the church" (Littel, *op. cit.* 1977). Even this Hitler rejected. For the first time in the long history of the persecution of Jews, Jews had no alternative. Their Jewish birth was their ticket to the lethal chambers of Auschwitz or to the gallows or open pits.

15. Hilberg, Robinson, Poliakov, etc.

16. Richard L. Rubenstein: *After Auschwitz.*

17. *Ibid:* Chapter 1.

18. L. Poliakov: *The Harvest of Hate.*

19. Rubenstein: *op. cit.,* page 3.

V

THE COMPLAINT AGAINST HEAVEN

> This is the story of a Ghetto that was nearing its end, and about a Shames (Synagogue Sexton) who began losing his sanity. The Shames used to storm into the Synagogue every morning, ascend the pulpit, and call out aloud. He would begin with restraint but then proceed with anger: "I came to inform Thee, Master of the Universe, that I am here!"
>
> Came the first slaughter followed by many more. The Shames somehow managed to survive each of them unharmed, and after each of these terrifying round-ups, he would break into the Synagogue, bang with his fists on the table and shout as loudly as he could: "Thou seest, Master of the Universe, I am still here!"
>
> After the final slaughter he remained the only one in the desolated Synagogue. He was the last Jew who remained alive. For the last time he ascended the pulpit, raised his eyes to the Holy Ark, mumbled a few blessings and cried out: "Thou seest, I am still here!" He remained silent for a moment and then added chokingly and in a voice full of sadness, "But Thou, where art Thou?"
>
> Elie Wiesel, "Musaf Lanoar," *Hadoar*

Putting God on trial is not a rare phenomenon in the life of Judaism. The Jews, as a "God-intoxicated" people from the very beginning of their distinct existence, did not spare their praises for the Maker and were not bashful about challenging God's seeming injustice. Nor did the Jews retreat from their intrepid position of protest against malevolence in the world. The ambiguity of the concept of God's nature and His role in man's affairs is such in Judaism that it affords the faithful Jew the possibility of leveling his complaint against heaven if and when it is done within the context of honesty. God can be challenged for permitting sadism, wickedness and treachery to pervade humankind.

The grievance is not capricious. Its propriety is derived from the theological proposition that God is omnipotent, omniscient and omnipresent. It assumes that He is the only and final arbiter in all matters. He is author of the ethical laws and commandments and as the Master of the Universe, He metes out rewards and punishments to each in accordance with each person's behavior. Understandably, the divine concept of reward and punishment is often incomprehensible to man's human perception. This is why man had difficulty in reconciling the eternal contradiction of "The righteous suffer and the wicked prosper".[1]

Furthermore, if we assume that God determines even a man's "lifting of his finger",[2] how can it be declared that man is morally a free agent and that man has freedom of choice?[3] And if we acquiesce to the proposition that freedom of choice is an absolute mandate granted to man from creation, how is then to be understood the nature of God's providence over the individual in particular and the human collective in general?

Again, if everything is preordained then there is no justification in our fulminations against our verdict from Above. However, if there is free will and there is no predetermined verdict against man from heaven, then there is no justification for complaining against God. Man has to turn inwards, search his own ways and that of his fellow man, and blame himself for his doleful predicament and for the troubles that descend upon him from his own kind. Among the many Divine attributes there is also the highest attribute of the *Summum Bonum* which proposes that God is good and that God created a good world "and the Lord saw it and it was good" and man was given the choice to fructify and improve the world or to devastate God's beautiful garden on earth. Either man can join in partnership with God or go his own separate way and cancel out God's very intent to humanize and civilize human society and live with the consequences.[4]

The poetry which encompasses the refutation of theodicy is predicated, however, upon the assumption that God is omnipotent. Consequently, "His guilt is inexcusable" for His part in the

Holocaust, albeit, for the sake of argument, as a passive onlooker. Instead of interceding, so goes the argument, He remained detached, thus allowing the incomprehensible and despicable sadistic slaughter of His people whom He chose as His witnesses among men.

There are also those among the poets who negate God's existence altogether. They reinstate Him for the sake of using Him as a target, as it were, for their argumentative attacks, since without a God Who personified justice and the highest moral good, their accusations would make no sense. There are others who maintain that God does exist but deny Him providential powers. There are those who insist on God's existence in spite of their gnawing doubts for otherwise, without faith in the divine presence, there would be no meaning to survival, continuation and the future of man and of Judaism. Still others remain in an agnostic shock-amazement, too numb to formulate their conception of the Holocaust apocalypse. There are those who see the Holocaust as the fulfillment of a preconceived divine plan, the culmination of evil which is to usher in the "commencement of the process of redemption", a price our historic destiny is supposed to exact for our national rejuvenation and the restoration of national sovereignty in the Land of our Fathers. The most perturbing view seems to be that of *Limitatio Dei,* that is to mean, God exits but He is impotent in the face of evil and that God too is subject to His own limitations . . . theologically it is untenable and rationally inadmissable . . .

The preceding summary outlines the ramifications of the continuous unsettled theological argument of the post-Holocaust era. On these argumentations, concepts and hypotheses rest Holocaust literature in general and poetry in particular. These weighty contentions serve as the basis for the protest within the raging indictment as voiced by Yitzchak Sela in his poem, "Reb Levi Yitzchak":

> The Lord of Hosts sits in heaven
> And looks on in silence . . .
> But I,
> I refuse to be silent . . .

Poetry is multifaceted and contains a variety of forms, not only in its criticism but also in the very language of its complaint. For this reason, the thematic genre across the entire gamut of poetry is both interconnected and difficult. Yet one must beware of falling into the trap of exaggeration. Hence, the "blasphemous" language that is prominently noticed, should not be summarily dismissed or condemned. It does not, in the final analysis, transgress the limits of respectful propriety. Above every stanza and verse hover profound love and deep-seated faith. If we encounter raging language, it is the spontaneity of outburst from the depths of disappointment in God's seeming indifference, resulting from the encompassing sorrow that in the hour of supreme crisis God's redeeming arm did not come to our rescue.

It should be noted that disillusionment and disappointment in God reflect the quintessence of criticism, rather than outright heresy. Perhaps Elie Wiesel was on target in exposing this particular paradox in the entire theological complexity of on the Holocaust issue from which there is no escape hatch:

> You are blaspheming he repeated gently, as if he were envious, as if he would have liked to blaspheme as well! God's final victory, my son, lies in man's inability to reject Him. You think you're cursing Him. But your curse is praise; you think that you are fighting Him, you think you're crying out your hatred and rebellion, but all you're doing is telling Him how much you need His support and forgiveness.[5]

In an address Wiesel delivered on April 27, 1976, in Philadelphia, he said ". . . this event of the Holocaust could not have been without God, nor could it have been with God. It cannot be conceived on any level."[6] With the last statement Wiesel focuses upon the prevailing trend of thought of the Holocaust and post-Holocaust literature.

It is of great importance to realize that Jewish history actually has been produced in historiographical writings for most of Jewish existence. The awareness of the importance of recording our history was already mentioned in the Talmud. Rabbi Shimon Ben Gamliel said: "We too cherish the (memory) of our troubles, but what can we do? For the moment we sit down to write them down *Eyn Anu Maspikin* . . . (other events occur which we do not manage to write about) (T.B. Shabbat 136). Our lachrymose history never ceased and somehow it was interwoven into the writings of its own time, directly or indirectly. One important thing, however, has always taken place after every event of our people's momentous suffering. After every destruction a vast and prolific literature sprung into being. After the First Temple's destruction (586 B.C.) the composition of the Pentateuch was finalized and followed by the final redaction of the "Prophets" and "Writings." After the destruction of the Second Temple (70 C.E.) the Mishnah was composed, and finalized by the middle of the thrid century. By the end of the sixth century the Talmud was concluded, and it was sealed by the time the Islamic fury was unleashed in the middle of the seventh century. After the expulsion from Spain (1492) the Kabbalistic Literature was fully expanded and the Shulchan Aruch [The Compendium of the Codex of Jewish Law by Rabbi Joseph Karo (1488-1575)] appeared. The common denominator of this curious phenomenon has been the preservation of the accumulated knowledge and ideas which Judaism produced in the crucible of its historical experiences and which secured the continuation of the authentic spirit of Jewish tradition. In addition, within this literature we find expression of the events that took place and even interpretations of the events with excruciating pangs, giving reasons why the Gates of Heaven were sealed and the alarming outcry was unheeded. This was the nature of our entire literature as reflected in the elegiac threondies, lamentations and *piyutim* of many centuries.[7]

The first to set the trend of dialogue with God was Abraham, in the days of Sodom and Gomorrah's impending doom, who inveighed: "Will not the judge of righteousness of the universe mete out justice?" (*Genesis* XVIII:22) The prophets and psalmists followed suit in crying out:

How long will I implore Thee
And Thou hearest me not
How long will I cry to Thee
About the committed violence
And Thou helpest me not? . . .

— *Habakuk* I:2-3

Why, O, Lord, Thou standest afar
And hidest in times of trouble?

— *Psalm* X:10

Our sages, evidently at a moment of great national distress, could not continue their forebearance and imputed in a scathing metathetical paraphrasing of: "Mi Kamochah Ba'eylim Adonai" (Who is like unto Thee, O Lord, among the gods) by transposing "Ba'eylim" into

"Ba-ilmim" meaning "mutes." Hence they obtained a new reading: "Who is like unto Thee among the mutes," who is like unto Thee who hears about the annihilation of your children and keeps quiet? . . .

As we can see, the Jewish people with their leaders, poets, and writers, raised their voice of protest against Heaven without haughtiness but with the deep hurt of heartfelt disillusionment. At the same time they held on to Him tenaciously and argued with Him in the spirit of the Berdichover Rebbe's Din-Torah with God Almighty . . . It is not a litigation in the coloquial understanding of the term. It is a symbolic but powerful public demand from God to admit *a priori* the Jewish people's intrinsic righteousness; in the Jewish people's rightful indignant rejection of any wrong committed to deserve such cruel and barbaric punishment. The *mea culpa* tune that reverberated throughout Jewish literature has totally disappeared from the vocabulary of the Holocaust victims or vicarious witnesses. This is a didactic lesson of far-reaching consequences. This sort of mood must be remembered by those theologians who prefer to be rejected rather than confront the radical metamorphosis in theology in the post-Holocaust period.

The Jewish theological stance within the Holocaust literature takes on a new physiognomy. It spells out a total rejection of the slightest intimation of accepting any culpability, in the religious sense, which could have resulted in such severe suffering. Nothing of the sort. We hear no longer *Al Cheyt Shechatanu Lefanecha* (For the sins we have committed against Thee); we hear instead a counter-attack: *Al Cheyt Shechatata Lefaneynu* . . . (For the sin Thou hast committed against us . . .) The argument counters with a reprimand: the severity of the Holocaust could never be justified vis-a-vis our wrongdoing. We could never have transgressed so much to deserve it. Thusly we are righteous and innocent and wronged, and entitled to bring God to trial regardless of the proposition or defense: "That God's ways are not the same as man's . . ."[9]

Yet, even though this has remained a predominant mood, it needs to be emphasized that alongside this mentioned "mood" a unique dominant trait remained in the thinking of Holocaust and post-Holocaust literature. Wiesel's complaint led the way with its contention: that man is capable of tolerating a God Who has created murderers who could and would murder for sheer pleasure. The Jews, throughout their long centuries of suffering in the Diaspora, have adjusted their thinking to accept suffering whilst being committed to God Who chose them from among the nations also for the unique distinction to be slaughtered for His esoteric reasons . . . However, to reject God or negate His existence, the Jew would lose his ground for existence. Thus, it is preferable to suffer, to challenge, to blaspheme, to villify, and curse, even to go insane and be murdered, rather than to admit even to oneself, in one's own privacy: There is no God, God is dead.[10]

In view of the aforementioned, the "Accusatory Motif" of Holocaust poetry is characteristically infused and suffused with a self-reproaching reaction. Its attitude is derived from the psychological tension which creates spontaneous reactions without rational cogency. It reflects hesitancy and a certain imbalance across the entire spectrum. It is oft times contradictory while encompassing all the arguments and settling for none. It is accusatory, defensive, blasphemous, remorseful, heretical and deeply religious, a spectacular conglomeration of ideas vying in an internal struggle for a definition:

Alas, how can I look into
Your pure and holy smile,
Whilst between me and God
There is ill-feeling?

— David Shimoni

The heart of the Holocaust poet is enraged and furious. He is self-chastising and befuddled. His raging soul renders him restive and flings him about in all directions: from faith to heresy and from heresy to faith. In one breath he simultaneously deplores and says:

You have satiated me with bitterness,
You have quenched me with wormwood.

— *Lamentations* III:15

And then he comforts himself and declares:

God's kindness does not cease
Because His compassion never ends.

— Ibid III:22

This sort of mental frustration permeates our entire reflective literature from Bible times to the present.

The accusatory motif against Heaven in modern Hebrew literature appeared for the first time in its sharpest form at the time of the Kishinev Pogroms of 1903 in the Ukraine. Bialik, Tschernichovsky, Shneur, Shimoni and others reacted with particular vehemence, followed by a chain reaction of devastating nihilistic inferences which left no room for much of a discussion in the area of theodicy. It is clear, that they took an undaunted position and voiced their indictment and the way they felt. They stormed, shouted, incited and rebelled. They rallied the people to hear their bitter grievance against God in a language unheard heretofore in our national literature: "No God, No King, No Hero" proclaimed David Shimoni, leaving no room to add anything else.

In order to facilitate the understanding of the theological difficulties with which poetry contended, we have subdivided the subject into separate themes according to particular theological issues which dominate the poetry of the Holocaust, as well as the Holocaust literature *in toto.* They are:

1. "There is no judgment nor is there a judge"
2. God's indifference to His people's extermination.
3. God is not omnipotent.
4. The challenge from within faith.
5. Protest against God's hiding His face (Deus Obsconditus).

1. There Is No Judgment Nor Is There A Judge

From a psychological point of view, denying God seems to be a natural reaction under given circumstances of duress and terror. Consciously and subconsciously the Jew was hoping for God's intervention exactly in that supreme fateful hour of his struggle. Since this hope did not come true, out of complete despair this outcry broke forth:

> . . . And there is no longer a father
> Who personally will nullify our verdict
> And there is no God who will hear us
> And have compassion upon his children.
>
> — Binaymin Tene, "Yaldut"

It depends, of course, on who says it and how it is said . . . The disaster alarm came spontaneously without restraint. This is why the moralistic dictum in the Talmud; not to judge a person in the hour of grief, applies doubly to the poets who sincerely eulogized their people's lot. Tschernichovsky's pessimism is thus defined in his poem, "The Murdered of Sirmonia."

There is no God, indeed, there is none!
If there is God, didn't He see
The injustice and terrible violence
Perpetrated by man against man
In His name and in His honor?
There is no God in heaven —
There is no God!
A God in heaven . . .? And He didn't hear
My anguished moans,
The cry of my prayer
From the one who was calling to Him
While choking on the gallows
With the last thought
O my gasping breath? . . .
No! There is no God!

Some may consider the poet's charges too hasty in his anticipated judgment, for he died in 1943. But unfortunately no one can deny that Tschernichovsky wrote his charges as if he saw in his poetic vision the destruction of the Jewish world in Europe and that his people were alone, abandoned. Is there a prescribed limit to one's reaction in a time of such grief?

If there be found someone who doubts poetic extra-sensory perception, will he then doubt, too, Yitzchak Katzenelson, an eyewitness to the Holocaust and its martyred victim? How ought we read his accusation against Heaven as he addressed the issue with majestic simplicity and scintillating sarcasm:

This is how it all began
Right from the start . . .
Heavens, tell me please, why?
Tell me for what reason
Did we have to die?
Why do we deserve to be insulted,
Alone of all this vast universe?
So mute and deaf is this earth

As if it closed its eyes for good . . .
But you great skies
You didn't close your eyes.
You saw what was happening from above
And it didn't sicken you?
It didn't enrage you at all,
The slaughter of my people
The very best,
And you didn't even turn
Upside down on your heads?

Woe, why are you so blue
You skies of blue,
Why are you so beautiful
When we are being slaughtered?

I call upon all the prophets from their graves
And I adjure them: See, I implore you!
Look up to your bright skies
And spit into their faces!
Tell them: The hell with you!
Be forever accursed!

You, heavens, beheld from above
When on foot, by train or on water
In brightly clear days and
In the darkness of night
The children of my people
Were transported to their death.
A million children have they murdered
But your heart did not move
Nor your compassion . . .
Millions of noble mothers and
Fathers did they kill too,
And you didn't tremble
Nor did your skin quiver a bit . . .
And you looked on . . .
You certainly have no God
Within your heavens,
You are a deceit, you're absurd!
You have no God within you anymore!

Open the gates ye heavens

Open them broad and wide,
And let in all my slaughtered children
Of my tortured and tormented people.
Open your gates for the mass ascent to heaven
An entire crucified nation,
Heavily pained will enter your realm.
Alas, each one of my slaughtered children,
Merits to be a God unto himself!
Woe, heavens so desolate and abandoned
The firmament wide, empty and still,
My only God, I lost in you,
But for them it was not enough
They wanted a trinity . . .
The Jewish God was not enough
They wanted His spirit
And the Galilean crucified Jew too.
They sent us all up to heaven
A heathen ritual vile and contemptible
Rejoice ye heavens and celebrate!
Impoverished you were, now, you became rich,
You had a blessed harvest
An entire people, what luck you have!
Rejoice ye heavens, with your Germans above,
And the Germans will rejoice with you down below,
And let a fire burst out from the ground upon you
And a fire from you shall
Consume the entire surface of the earth.

— "The Song of the Slaughtered Jewish People"

We ought to pay attention to another poet whose voice of grief came from the outside, yet whose words reflect an empathy with the mood of those lugubrious days. The obvious difference in the indictment that comes from the Nazi victim himself and the complaint of the mourner for the Holocaust who was not there, is in the degree of intensity. The outsider's intensity was greater and his condemnation louder and freer. The victim's voice was subdued by despair and by deep cutting refutation.

The world is lawless! And the sheep is torn apart
In vain does one desperately seek help around
But no rescue is to be found.

And the fool is surprised:
That he found in the field of Cain
The bones of Abel as fertilizer
Look at people behind you
A community of skeletons.
Are these the criminals
Are these the sinners?

We have erred with our fathers,
There is no justice and there is no judge.
And he who has a weapon in his hand
Can kill and decapitate at will . . .

— Avraham Schwartz, "Shirim"

These are not elegiac epigrams, empty declarations or bombastic accusations. Therein we find doubt and denial: "We have erred with our fathers/There is no justice nor judge." Or in Greenberg's version: "Where is the God of the Jews?", is not a matter of innocent inquiry. We hear here a definitive judgment: "There is none" . . . This sort of denial is by far not philosophical but rather symptomatic, pointing to man's despair of the Creation and his Creator, and as a confirmation of the supposed fatalism in our people's lot from which there is no escape:

I know, I know this,
You are no longer God! . . .
The doors up on High
Stand wide open
Prayers die out
In the blood of the maimed . . .
Even your hosts in heaven
Disobey Thy commands —
Since day pronounced death,
Day was summoned for judgment . . .

— Yitzchak Ivri, *Beyn Dam Ledam,*
"Introductory Note"

And more than the declared fatalism is the proclaimed nihilism:

There is no God, neither Hebrew nor Christian!

There is no God, because he is not — indeed! . . .
There is no God in the world,
And perhaps neither a Satan.
But there is . . . there is a world
Woe unto me —
A world of falsehood and lie.

— Tschernichovsky, "The Murdered of Sirmonia"

It is evident that Tschernichovsky despairs of God altogether; therefore, his language is declarative and unembellished. The poets Uri Tzvi Greenberg and Meir Mohar are by far not ready to play the coroner. Their deep-seated faith allows them, rather, to be sarcastic and argumentative. They try, in a sense, to hit back . . .

Greenberg's argument has a novel twist. He declares that the Gentiles have a God, not the Jews. Had the Jews a God of their own, He would have prevented their extermination the way the Gentiles were spared:

. . . For You, O Lord,
There are none others but the Gentiles.
Fortunate are they who are alive . . .

They have always considered You to be their Lord!

And now they have been persuaded
The Jews have no God . . .
Only the living Gentiles pray to You now
O Lord . . .
You are being called: The Gentile God!
There are no longer any Jews in Gentile lands.
They have been convinced alright
That You are all theirs . . .

— "Rechovot Hanahar"

Mohar is more plaintively accusatory:

Upon our back they have ploughed
And You Lord have kept Your silence!
Our martyrs inquired of You
But You have not responded!

From the land of the living they were uprooted
And You, O Lord, failed to rush to their rescue.
Those who were ready to die for Your sake were expelled
And You, O Lord, did not even sanctify their name.
Rejoice in Your Gentiles, Lord,
They have replaced Your people
Whom You have abandoned!

— "Ve'ata Elohim"

2. God's Indifference to His People's Extermination

The tragic events have led some of the generation's outstanding poets to project, as it were, a pathological outrage which seemingly prevents any sort of reconciliation with God and His judgment. David Shimoni demonstrated a gradual unbending attitude since the pogroms in the Ukraine. He isolated himself within the cubicle of his own bitter disappointment in God Who, as he experienced it, demonstrated no mercy when his people were in need of Him, and therefore denounced any possibility of an "I-Thou" relationship. He went as far in his initial persistence to reject even his mother's pleas to recite *Kaddish* after her death. His rebelliousness is sevenfold greater than his love for his mother as he burst out in a scathing indictment:

He murdered,
He tortured,
He fed dogs
With the flesh of innocent children,
How can then, I, say:
"Yitgadal Vyitkadash"
Magnified and sanctified be Thy name.

— *Shirim,* Vol. II

Such language found its way into the thought vocabulary of Holocaust literature during and after the *Shoah*. Its beginnings go back to the beginning of this century and although the bruising expressions fell like heavy hammer blows upon the Jewish community, the poets did not diminish the pressure of their protestations, continuing right into the Holocaust era.

There is, however, an essential difference. When the Kishinev pogroms broke out the world protested. The global reactions were loud and clear. The circumstances of the *Shoah* were totaly different. It came upon us from a different set of political, economic and social conditions which on the surface did not indicate initially the possibility of such an annihilation and, therefore, it caused an irreparable shock to man and culture. The dimensions were also much different and the degree of world reaction was scandalously so depressing, that it compelled Shimoni to ask in utter perplexity:

> Every voice and sound
> Are suffocated in the throat,
> Every whisper and expression
> Melt away and disappear,
> Every cry and dirge
> Turn into mute silence —
> Every lament startles
> But God, no one hears . . .

And he repeats once more:

> Master of all souls
> Where,
> Where art Thou?

But since God's reply did not come, the poets themselves offered the answer. They spoke out of their own woe and pain, from what they saw and witnessed. They saw and willingly concluded: If God exists and did not prevent the horrible slaughter, it is perhaps none more than His will. Without any restraint they served Him up what was due Him in accordance with their perception:

> May the smoke ascend into the heavens today
> And may it reach Thy nostrils
> The fumes of the sheep
> From the cities of slaughter —
> The cloud of incense
> From suffocating gases
> The reeking stench of
> Tens of thousands of Your sons
> Corpses which were
> Sacrificed before Your eyes.
> The tears of prayer You rejected

Refused to listen to the cry against violence,
The moan of terror You did not hear
From the mouth of suckling babes.
For a slaughtered offering You have yearned —
Complete, total,
On all of Your altars.
Yes? And therefore . . .
May my eternal silence
Today ascend to Your heavens
And reach Your ears
That dead-silence . . .
And this calmness of the grave
Should be so oppressive to Thy ear
That You will not be able to bear
Even the slightest sound!
Blood upon blood! —
How many are the streams
Which render every nuance red . . .
For Thy silence is Thy praise?
Yes? And therefore —
May it ascend to Thy ears
This silence of my blood, of the grave.

— M.Sh. Ben-Meir, "Yaaleh"

The accusation cannot be more direct: "For a burnt offering You yearned/You wanted it complete . . ./Upon each of Your altars . . ." Simultaneously, with the indictment of God, personal guilt disappears. We hear total rejection of any responsibility which would have otherwise been punishable but not to the degree of suffering which God supposedly unleashed upon his people:

As long as the pulse will beat in my heart,
As long as I don't know why and what for
Thou hast caused all this to happen,
Forget I cannot,
Forget, I will not . . .!

— Shimoni, *op. cit*

After all, how can an entire people forget when one of every three Jews was mercilessly slaughtered? Assuming we have transgressed against God's moral and ethical behest, how can we forget the indescribable annihilation or our children which is beyond atonement? "You have exterminated suckling babies who have not sinned/And those who have just been weaned/And did not yet sin . . ." And what about God's own bookkeeping? How is the Lord balancing His grand account with His "Chosen" people?

My Lord, I didn't audit Your blazing record
Wherefrom Your stamp-of-truth is shining forth.

Nor am I, mortal, pretending
To uncover the script or resolve the mystery . . .
All that I want to know is:
Why have You dealt Your people such an awful blow?
I cannot perceive,
The loftiness of Your divine reason,
My brain has been blinded from the horror of
Your strokes
But, before darkness covers me,
One of a thousand, answer, I beg Thee,
My children who were strangled, crushed,
and drowned
Tell me please: These innocent sheep
What sin have they committed?

— Ibid

These perturbing and gnawing accusations remain suspended in the atmosphere that envelops the total Jewish being: heart, soul, and spirit. Doubt eats into the marrow of one's faith. God seems to have denied us the ability to resolve this question of questions once and for all. If we only knew the reason, how much easier it would have been to carry our burdens of tragedy and annihilation. God has, as it were, withdrawn His compassion and made sure that His verdict will be fully executed upon His people. Nothing is left to the poet but to hurl back his indictment at God. But to no avail. The Lord remained silent and irresponsive within His protective isolation. The poet establishes his case, painful as it is:

And the survivor is challenging
Voicelessly but with determined vigor,

But most dreadful of all,
There is no one to complain to or to call out to.

— Shimoni, "V'eleh Toldot Ud"

Indeed, one's personal nightmare is oppressive: Is God guilty? And perhaps more frightening: Perhaps there is none to complain to?

3. God Is Not Omnipotent

The speculation around *Limitatio Dei,* the assertion that God suffers from limitations, has arisen within theology in the theory of theodicy. Theologically, God's all-encompassing absolute and infinite omnipotence asserts itself inductively and deductively from the very definition of God as creator and the most perfect being. However, when God's omnipotence is viewed from the premise of theodicy, namely, from the definition of God's justice in creating the world and the justification of His deeds, an acute problem arises when the phenomenon of evil is scrutinized.

The argument thus runs along the following line of thinking: If God is the Creator of the universe and everything within it, then evil must have been part of creation. It would also follow that evil functions only at the exclusive behest of God. If so, how is it that evil is so uncontrollably rampant and inexplicably cruel? For if evil is functioning under the divine aegis, then God is responsible for the dominion of evil in the world. It obtains that He who is supposed to be merciful, just and patient, would not allow such profound and horrific cruelty as the Holocaust massacres to be unleashed upon man. Moreover, since God is omnipresent, namely, simulatneously immanent and transcendental, He is equally omniscient and expected to know the anguish of man's suffering wherever man is oppressed and tortured. Thus His providential arm and intervention is therefore expected since He is seen as the Master who metes out His retributive wrath for unjustly wronging His creatures. This is inferred from His infinite attribute of mercy . . .

The difficulty is quite obvious. Some philosophers attempted to solve the problem of evil by redefining evil as the absence of good. But others, aware of the logic of the argument and unable to absolve God from having created evil, propose that since God endowed man and Satan with a free spirit, evil therefore may appear capricious, unpredictable and strikingly inexplicable. This casuistry evades the heart of the argument by irrational rationalization of the phenomenon of evil. Our sages in the Talmud had the courage to intimate their great difficulty to explain the reality of evil and the obscurity of its source.[11]

God in Judaism is not an Aristotelian "unmoved mover." He is an active, creative, concerned, compassionate and forebearing God. Man can avert evil decrees against himself through prayer, charity and repentance. God is expected to listen to man's supplications. The efficacy of prayer is basic to the relationship between man and God and God's response and intervention is expected in return.[12]

Where then was God when we desperately cried out to Him from the depths of our suffering, from the gallows, the gas chambers, the forests and ravines? There must be an explanation! Perhaps God's power is limited? For how otherwise would He allow such mass assassinations, conceived and sealed by January 20, 1942, at the Grossen-Wannse Nazi Ministerial Conference, to go into full operation?[13]

This is how the entire argument evolves in its own subjective framework of reference.

Poets and poetry are far from being involved in rational speculation. Poetry reacts to a gut-feeling. It speaks for and with the people. It is emotional and sensitive and holds up the sincere belief of the victims as its basic premise upon which its entire argument rests. It tenaciously refuses to let God, so to say, "off-the-hook" in these anguish laden reflections. Poetry here refuses to philosophize insouciantly on this painful and stirring problem. It rather ontologicaly assesses the stark facts of the Holocaust and emotionally cries out against the injustice and even allows sympathy for God's seeming limitations. To be sure, poetry may take on different forms but it retains its basic contention. Poetry's anger and bitterness aims persistently to question God's omnipotence and His mercy and to decry the abandonment of the victims languishing in torture whose cry He did not heed. In short, Hebrew poetry refuses to skirt the painful issue. It struggles with the issue as best it can. Thus speaks Bailik in the days of Kishinev, a veritable forerunner of Holocaust poetry:

> Forgive me you wretched of the world,
> Your God is as poor as you.
> He is poor in your lifetime

And no less when you die.
For if perchance you come tomorrow
To demand your reward,
Knock on My doors, I'll welcome you:
Come in and see, I am bankrupt!
And I am so sorry for you, My children
And My heart goes out to you:
To your dead — Who died in vain . . .
Neither I, nor you, did ever know
Why you died or for whom
And there is no sense to your death
As there was no meaning to your life.
And the Lord, what does He say?
He hides His head in the cloud
And [in view] of pain and shame
Departs embarrassed . . .

— "Ba'ir Hahareyga"

This is a classical example of the sort of sarcasm that exposes directly the particular aspect of divine weakness which was assumed to be our detriment. B. Mordecai thus concludes his poem in the same genre:

I regret all the martyrdom
For the sake of Heaven.
I came to tell You Lord,
We served You in vain . . .

— "B'Har Ha'elohim"

Extreme disappointment begot mental depression in those who believed "in perfect faith" that Divine rescue would come and in the hour of "be or not to be" it did not appear:

Isn't it so my God?
When in trouble
In disgrace or disease
We are together?
And therefore —
And therefore calamity won't frighten me
I shall be taken away,

Only with You beside me,
Isn't it so, my Lord?

— A. Hameiri, *Hamoked Haran*

And in a moment of madness, the poet is led to the conclusion that perhaps the world is ruled by an impotent Master:

Perhaps You too are with us in the stocks?
Perhaps it is not a children's game
But Your impotence that
Dragged You in with us
Into the turbulent vortex . . .

— "Bamaarbolet"

And perhaps it is so? Perhaps God was incapable of controlling the situation . . . But this aspect does not deter the poet, especially when he is stricken with grief and humiliation for the catastrophe that befell his people. He persists, in fact, with asking whether there is indeed a Master of the Universe; and if He does exist, does He possess the power to rule or is He ruled by others. Between the two opposing poles and in the straits of delusion the poet quivers, his lament unanswered, finally forced to declare:

Don't yell, don't cry,
Stop the blood,
And speak to God
As you converse with
Any human being —

— Hameiri, Ibid

This seems to mean: treat God as if He is endowed with human attributes and relate to Him as a ruler with finite powers. It is indeed a rebellious voice, that resounds from "A naked heart, tired and sad/Which emits all the despair/Wrath and horror/protruding like piercing nails . . ./."

Accordingly, the indictment and declaration of God's limitations are an expression of mourning and empathy with God's plight. In a sense an awareness of a painful fact:

I know, O Lord, Thy countenance
Is turned towards me,
I, among the most lonesome
The last of Jewish remnants,
I am Your destroyed Temple's
Last remaining wall.
Descend please from the dark cloud
Come down and pray before me
Offer Your dirge
Before my stones
Cry, O Lord, Thy cry! . . .

— Aharon Zeitlin, "Mimkomcha El Mistatrim"

The poet regrets God's good intentions, for he was unable to help his people. Therefore, the tables are turned. The pardoner is told to ask pardon. The argument has finally been turned on its head.

In a similar vein, Enda Finkerfield Amir turns to God and says: "Thank You very much! I forego all the privileges of rejoicing in the beautiful world which You have created. After this horrendous massacre, Your world remains nothing but a cruel, inhuman, wicked slaughter-house":

Be ashamed, dishevel Your hair,
Confess before me,
I have a heart,
In it I contained Your world.
But You,
In this forest
Are acting boisterously . . .

— "Gadish"

This frontal assault upon God's limitations, as it were, is relentless. Zalman Shneur raised this attack to the level of biting satire. In his poem "Rabbi Levi Yitzchak of Berdichov's New Argument" he confronts God on the basis of Jewish history. He proves the righteousness of the Jewish people who kept their fidelity with God and retained their trust in His promise, despite much suffering, that His people would receive ample reward in the "world to come". However, the *Shoah* descended upon it and ended all its dreams and visions of the future. The Jewish people were pushed to the edge of the precipice of no return. And Rabbi Levi Yitzchak, the legendary defender of his people in Israel, advances his extreme and catagorical demand from God:

> Reward Your children
> Now, and at once!
> Or,
> Admit publicly
> Before the entire holy congregation
> That You are bankrupt, as it were,
> That You have lost all Your potentialities
> Of divine power.
> That You lost Your majesty
> And hide Yourself in the cloud . . .

Shneur compassionately continues to assure the Lord, that despite the great disappointment, the Jewish people will not abandon or forsake their God. Shneur is even ready to forgive all the outstanding divine obligations toward Israel, in order to prevent His enemies from deriding Him. But the fulfillment of Israel's promises to God is predicated upon one condition, that He save His people right now, or admit that He is bereft of power:

> I implore Thee, this evening
> By the light of the many memorial candles
> Tell the truth! . . . And we
> Will remove all Your outstanding obligations
> I, Levi Yitzhak, the son of Sarah,
> Of the holy congregation of Berdichov
> Am first to forgive . . .

Yet, there is a curious sense of compassion and ethical sensitivity which spills over into the raging argument in its anthropomorphic treatment of God. No matter how heated and volatile the argument may be on the theological level, Judaism's ethics still govern its spirit. Our sages, discussing God's attributes, wished to derive a didactic lesson. For example, they said: "Since God is compassionate, so you ought to be compassionate . . ." (*T.B. Shabbat,* p. 133a). Thus the poets reversed the case in confronting "the helpless" God . . . Although He could not have compassion upon His people, His people have enough compassion to have pity on Him. This is how the desperate sick little boy cries out in frustration:

Master of the Universe
I have compassion
Upon You —
How come,
You have no compassion
On me? . . .

— David Shimoni, "Misipurei Na'ar Choleh"

The same is true for the poet who, adroit in his biting criticism and challenge, knows also how to cry over his God who seems to have lost His hegemony over His creation and creatures:

And perhaps You are with us
In the stocks?
In times of trouble
We have always called upon Thee,
But if You linger with us in the stocks
To whom shall we cry for help?

— Avigdor Hameiri

That was the most painful aspect. The poet was not eager to despair of his faith. He sought ways to find the proper address where to offer his supplications.

4. The Challenge From Within Faith

When we look into the essence and nature of this momentous quarrel with God in contemporary Hebrew poetery, we realize that our poets kept hold of the essential faith of Israel. Regardless of the particular forms of expression they chose, and in spite of their sometimes acrimonious tirades, they swung on the pendulum of their bruised souls, from one extreme to the other, encompassing the entire gamut of belief. There is no justification in accusing them in one sweeping critique of "frightful emptiness,"[14] or crediting them with exalted piety. In this whirlpool of mentally, psychologically and theologically frustrating confrontations with God and the Holocaust, the poets were searching for meaning, for some intelligible faith in

Israel's eternity, which could survive the fluctuating encounters of skeptcism. There is no reason to assume that despair dominated nor that faith was pervasive. Both moods prevailed and complemented each other in the days of our struggle for survival and on the way to our death.

In the following poem we obtain a glimpse into the world of "faith within resignation" through the saintly person of Reb Mendl, the brother of the famed and venerable "Rebbe" of the Gerer Chassidic Dynasty.

> . . . Reb Mendl washed his hands,
> And began with confession
> To the Master of the Universe
> And when the brutal Nazi commander
> Gave his order to open fire,
> Reb Mendl smiled toward Heaven,
> As if defying the last despair . . .
> . . . There is still a Jew
> Who sanctifies God's name
> A Jew who loves his brothers
> And subjugates malice and cruelty
> Even at the moment of death.

— Shin Shalom, "Reb Mendl"

In the following poem, here too, the Rabbi justifies God's will with love in the spirit of spiritual resistance, refusing to complain or even to protest against his Master of the Universe. This is the sort of heroism befitting Jewish martyrdom:

> . . . His eyelids are heavy and tired
> And they are closing by themselves
> But they see this wonderful ladder
> Stretching from the depths heavenward
> From darkness to splendor,
> On its steps ascend long lines of souls
> They ascend with joy and song toward the
> Heavenly gates
> His lips mutter:
> May His great kindness be blessed and glorified!
>
> We are guilty . . . we are rebellious . . .

For the sins we have committed . . .and as he was
Reciting
In silence the confessional . . .
And could not beat his breast
To fulfill custom's behest,
His chin he threshed on the ground
With every "Al-Cheit" another pound . . .

The tortureres his prayers were mocking
As his last spasm of life was weakening,
His being shaken from pain and woe,
He interrupted his silent meditation,
And opened his eyes and gazed at Heaven once more.

But to rage or fulminate he did not care
Nor roar with fury he would not dare:
O Lord of vengeance appear,
O Lord retaliate from up there!

— Ephraim Lisitzky, "The Rabbi Who
Was Buried Up to His Neck"

But along with unprecedented faith, there were also poets from whose heart broke forth alarming protest cries:

You stood calmly from afar
While my brethren were led to death.
Your mouth You muzzled from crying out
While they were lined up for dying.
You could have held out Your hand
And embraced them in Your bosom
When they were engulfed by flames
While in their last utterance, Thy name proclaimed.
O Lord, how will You exonorate the world?

— Sh. Shalom, "Reb Mendl"

The most outspoken and hard-hitting complaint was couched in familiar liturgical language.

. . . My God, how great is Thy wisdom
To torture the creatures of Thy handiwork —
My Lord, why do You rejoice in Your wrath

To frighten wretched man.
My faithfulness You exposed to ridicule
You removed the mask from Your kindness
And uncovered Your stern face
Mocking at the person in agony.
Woe, how God's love
Was transformed in me to ravenous hate
Which preys incessantly on my life
Like a lion on the scent of a cattleshed.

I am weary under Your constant scrutiny
Stop grinding my face.
The evening has come, let me go
With the useless entreaty of a complainer.
Lord, Who is to be implored
Does not want the sufferer's demise
He prefers his delirious indisposition.

— Meir Mohar, "Iyov"

Between the two horrific choices: either to pray hopelessly or to suffer deliriously, one can truly lose his sanity even among the most ardent and devout believers:

I am tired my Lord,
Too tired to carry on:
To search, to look
To dig into the secrets
And to understand nothing . . .

I am too weary to pray!
Even if I were to complain
With grinding of teeth
While raising eyes on high
I know of
Saintly poor Jews . . .
Who were dragged and beaten
Suffered and smitten,
Their wives and daughters
Violated before their eyes,
Their children slaughtered,
Torah Scrolls desecrated,
Their eyes pierced,

Their beard torn out . . .
Yet, Your blinded Jews
Were looking for You Lord!

And You, You heard,
You saw, and
Were not shaken!
Are You then wondering
Why man is despairing?
You know my Lord
That some remnant of faith in Thee
That once budded in me
Has not yet vanished . . .completely?

Nevertheless . . .
I am tired of this sickening situation,
To hope while in fear of extermination,
In the terrifying grime
Of reality's dunghill . . .

— Chaim Chamiel, "Moked V'nir"

This is the quintessence of the spiritual crisis *de profundis.* While not fully defined before the last Jew was murdered on the gallows, its symptoms were already well established in the transition period between degrading Ghetto life and agonizing death in Concentration Camps.

Let us turn to two poems written in the Ghetto. One was surely written by a young person. In great simplicity he unveils for us the horror, pain, fear, despair and faith in all their intensity. It is a representative chronicle of the Ghetto Jew's state of affairs. It is a chronicle in verse, an authentic document of an innocent witness and victim:

Around us are strong fortifications
Within their walls, Jews are living.
Mother!
Mother give me bread! I am hungry!
We all are so hungry!
We have no Messiah!
A week before Rosh Hashanah
The slaughter began.

Dark clouds spread over our heads
And Gentiles stood with rifles in their hands
Jewish possessions will soon be in their homes . . .
The end of the Jews has come,
Jews raised their hands in prayer to their God.
Woe unto all of us!
Thousands of Jews are being killed
Their blood like water is spilled.
Jews praying for the last time tried,
As loudly as they could, they cried.
Hear, Lord our God!
Save us from our enemies' rod!
But our God
Forgot
About our tragic lot!

— Eliyahu Zaretzki, "Geto Lachva"

The second poem was written by someone who lived by his faith but after reading it we may prefer to think that in his own pious way he was livid with rage:

I have not had any visions,
I am no prophet,
Neither in dreams have I seen anything
Nor have any secrets been disclosed to me.

I offered my prayers
To stars and to planets
Tell me when will an end come to our suffering?
How long will my persecuted people be
Dominated by the sword?

The clouds are dripping blood
To fertilize the furrow.
The moon is clad in red attire
To provide light for
The enemies in search
After my secret hideouts.
How long, how much longer?!
I sit and wonder:
You all must hate me from up yonder!
Plead, will You, for the children

Of Amram, the entire constellation —
They put us in chains
And the death dirge leads us on
And no one says a word, all is silent
Not a murmur nor a living vibration.
With lowered heads the
Celestial hosts
Wait for God's answer . . .

— Akiba Egozi, "Ad Matai?"

Thus the Ghetto poetry can be defined as the threnody of the unanswerable question . . . it is one long lachrymose dirge. The poets record in their elegies the fateful and ominous lot of European Jewry. It would be not only banal but cruel insensitivity, were one to analyze much of this poetry from a literary standpoint or evaluate its poetic craftsmanship. The alert, capable and consciously motivated victims tried to record everything and leave for the survivors a living document, a testament, a witness, both in prose and verse. Everything was hastily and surreptitiously recorded before capture by the firing squad or the hangmen. This was the poetic eulogy of a dying people's chronicle. It is the most exalted and purest expression of a murdered people's momentous reflection and meditation upon its life, destiny and message for those who may find it in the future. It serves as the phoenix-like voice of a never dying people, a source of scorn for a piously silent world, and a well of inspiration to assure Israel's continuation.

These words, verses and poems from the Ghetto and Concentration Camps, from the hideouts and partisans, were spontaneous explosions of an inner spiritual and emotional character. If misread or misunderstood they can be of shattering consequences. If understood, they become the elixir of our future life, the cornerstone, the foundation rock upon which to build and restore our Jewish future out of our own Holocaust ashes. No matter how seemingly blasphemous the questions sound, they should be perceived within the context of their unprecedented predicament of excruciating mental, physical and spiritual torture. This, I submit, was the fundamental motif of the particular poetry from within the Holocaust confines.

Two outstanding poems of high poetic level whose lack of "polished" artistic qualities points up their grandeur, authenticity, and great historic distinction and value, have made the sort of impact which has already catapulted them to the coveted title of "Epics" of the Holocaust. Yitzchak Katzenelson's "The Song of the Slaughtered Jewish People" is the more celebrated one. But the second, "Mima'amakim" (From the Depths) by Meir Bossak, is a worthy twin. Katzenelson's *magnum opus* is The Jeremiad of the Holocaust. Here the poet speaks "for" the slaughtered Jewish nation of Europe as a witness and victim. It is a chronicle of events and a testimony of its struggle and spirit.

Bossak's poem represents the unconquered Jewish soul. It is also the threnody of a destroyed people and a eulogy for a thousand years of spiritual history of a spiritually creative people in Exile, its uniqueness and its spiritual indestructability. Bossak's verse is permeated with profound faith. It is covered however with a veneer of contempt and scourging protest. It does not spare self-criticism nor does it lack implied Jewish hope. Bossak's particular form of protest is rooted in the internalized and unshakeable faith of the poet himself, who was from his early childhood deeply steeped in the profundity of traditional Judaism. Therefore there is the particular sensitivity, hurt and personal tragedy of a true believer who grapples with the imponderable postulates of faith. His accusation is laced with *Amore Dei.*

Bossak's criticism of his people, as he retrospectively dives into the events preceding the Nazi onslaught, is couched in the sympathetic terminology of an *Amicus Curiae* — yet upon the entire range of his topics hovers the spirit of a man who was there . . . He saw it, experienced it, was deeply scarred by it, but was never destroyed. He speaks with the voice of humility mixed with self assertion. In his youth he tried to touch the hem of the divine robe, but suddenly in the conflagration of the Holocaust he "Saw" God . . .

> . . . From the days when we walked before You,
> From the days of Isaac's binding . . .
> Thou knowest the inner thoughts of every man.
> O Lord, open my lips . . .!
> At night my bed — an altar — a knife
> And prayers for mercy.
> And by day — I am a wolf roaming,
> In snowy fields and forest —
> Stricken with hunger pangs

For Thy revelation
But I am lost, I stagger . . .
On behalf of the entire nation
That went up in fire like a golden sheaf
With the permission of the elders of Israel
Bowed down from Jewish suffering
. . . Weary of tests and challenges
With heads bowed from sorrow
Ascending the gallows with quiet dignity
"If this be God's will" . . .
On behalf of all the sainted martyrs
Who were sent to the abysses
Of blood and tears,
For the sin Thou hast committed against us . . .

The concluding verse of the introduction is the key to Bossak's quarrel with God. The underlying contention is: that not the people but God is called upon to avenge our humiliation and extermination, and He has to give His exalted answer as to why He visited so much calamity and trouble upon us. The poet buttresses his challenge by arguing that he was not among those who refuted Him. He remained His devoted servant.

All my life I ran after You
Like a dog after his master —
Now like a dog,
On the threshold of his house he rests,
And raises his head beholding devastated worlds.

And the blood of my yearnings
Led me all my life
Through the paths of my existence
To Thee . . .
And the Master, all He did
Was . . .
He kicked His dog . . .

How terrible and awful You are
And yet to Thee alone our eyes are turned
How then can You keep silent
When your fresh young garden is uprooted
From Your heavenly green coronet?

And if this was Your wish, Lord
Then extinguish the stars above my head . . .

And if we sinned —
After all, we were fashioned out of clay
O Lord,
On whom then are You taking revenge?

From the head adorned with T'fillin
A banner for the nations
Blood drips from its straps —
How can You look at it?
How come You have dispersed us in the world
Like sheep for the slaughter . . .?
We are suing You
Almighty —
For having sent us into the world,
Implanted in us a healthy instinct for life
And then handed us over to the slaughterer,
And we quivered in his hands,
While You Lord mocked us . . .
If the spider is condemned
For being created to devour the fly,
Why have You instilled in it
A desire to live
So that it quivers
In the spider's web?
And a sense of justice You have instilled in us,
In order that we can analyze,
Reason and know
And we immersed our heads in heavy thoughts
Until late at night
And dreams You made bloom
In the heart of man
About men of decency and heroism
Who fight for justice and the future of man
Until they came on the threshold of death —
There they discarded the pure visions
Of their hearts
In order to protect their still
Flickering life for one more day or hour,
Like worms they crawled
At the feet of the murderer
They begged and pleaded

And licked the dust of his boots
How degraded and despised we were
O Lord? . . .
For the sin You have committed
Against us . . .
For having us handed over
To the slaughterer
Like vermin in the walls of a house
Condemned to extermination —
For having instilled murderous
Proclivities in man
And then You mocked us
When You uncovered our inferiority.
Does the creator scorn
The ugliness of his own handiwork?
And You have demeaned us
In the dirt of the streets and in the
Dark cellars.

And they seized our children for slaughter
Like bedbugs.
And nations saw —
And nations kept their silence —
And nations enjoyed themselves
Because of the sins
Thou hast committed against us! . . .

— "Ve'ata Eynay Ra'atcha"

We deal here with a case of nihilistic denunciations. Yet the bridges of faith are not being burned down, nor is there any attempt to slam the door of authenticity of faith, deny our destiny, or reject our purpose. We have here a genuine insurrection by the most faithful. But there is no betrayal. There is real love and no hate. There is doubt but no distortion. We find here rich imaginative images out of our Jewish life that embrace our entire history and belief, interwoven with symbolism reaching deep into the heart of the Jewish essence. The raw material comes from the treasurehouse of our tradition, thus striking a deep chord in the Jewish heart. For this reason, this "would-be" quarrel with God retains its forcefulness, credibility and respect. It has all the attributes of a quarrel "within the family". Here, no one is a stranger. We are here on familiar grounds. The language itself is very suggestive, sharp as arrows aiming at an unmistakable target, God.

I believe in You, my Creator,
With perfect faith
The more You darkened our lives
The more You caused our fright
The more You continued to smite
With one slaughter after another
Here, there, everywhere
At the gates of the court
On the fence or on a layer of stones
And on the threshold of the hall
Inside and outside
And when my boiling blood was absorbed
Before cooling off;
Inasmuch as the pieces of my life quivered
Or were singed on the roasting pit.
And each piece screamed from the table
With a silenced mouth;
Inasmuch as Your wrath consumed
And denied survival of
Community after community
With its bundles of babes
In their bosoms;
Inasmuch as my groans day and night
While being bound
On the infernal slaughter table,
Were unheeded,
And instead
Embarrassed and slapped,
For Your failure to have mercy
Upon the bereaved
In the abyss of their grief;
Inasmuch as You exacted
The full harshness of Your verdict
And were incredibly cruel to me
You have even disgraced me for
Good measure . . .
Nevertheless,
I believe in You,
In the open or in a crevice of a rock
Where I may hide from Your shame

And in spite of Your
Having perverted my verdict
And being so cruel
I have trust in You . . .

— Yehudah Karni, "Shirim Min Hapinkas"

In the same genre we find the plaintiff's charges using the vocabulary of the Yom-Kippur liturgy:

. . . The day is almost gone
Your day, Lord, as well as mine,
A people is almost finished —
Your people, Lord, and mine —
For both of us
The time for "Ne'ilah" has arrived —
And woe unto us! . . .
You have killed my brothers,
You have put my sisters to death
And You had no mercy Father of Compassion
Not even on the babies, woe unto You!
Woe unto me! . . .
Woe unto You and me! . . .
How can the shame
Of Your pernicious destruction
Ever be atoned?
The man of faith — how can he still believe?
Who will cover up the blood
Of your victim? . . .

— M.Sh. Ben Meir, "Ne'ilah"

It seems that in the quarrel with God, the subject of the Holocaust afforded the faithful an opening wedge to break out from the pious sphere of stoic religiosity and from concern lest they be vexing to God. These words had to be heard and they were said with vigor and clarity in respectful language but with a vitriolic accent. This new accent and the change in terminology did betoken, after all, a change in thought and attitude which required a new vocabulary . . . Nevertheless, the most outstanding characteristic of the Hebrew poetic genius was that this poetry was grounded in the ethos of traditional Judaism. This intrinsic religious vein made all the difference in the impact that Hebrew poetry had upon our national awareness of the dimensions of the Holocaust.

> God, nothing bothers Him:
> Satan receives into
> His receptacle wide as the world
> The blood of an old man,
> A young maiden or a babe
> And he sprinkles the blood
> Upon God's altar, wide as the world,
> And God, nothing fazes Him:
> The lonely fallen on the battlefields
> And my brethren who were buried alive,
> Without going insane from their moans
> When they were digging their own graves
> In bitter frosty and starry nights
> Or in the burning sun.
> They despaired
> They despaired as I did
> In their horror, on the day of their murder.
>
> — Shimon Halkin, "Slichot 5703"

The poet truly believes that he is not negating God's existence. He only complains against God's "hiding His face," His silence or His severity in judgment against His people. Shimon Halkin offers here an additional nuance in the long tract of accusations against God. He proposes that "God doesn't care." It is a disturbing view, certainly inconsistent with the idea of an active, concerned and caring God. But in view of the Holocaust nightmare, in the tempest of utter frustration, resignation, shock, and despair, every idea or thought may or can be validated in the crucible of a world that went berserk in the pandemonium of horror in the human slaughterhouse, or in the open execution pit. When God is hiding, man is silent and ethics are suspended. Everything is possible and everything may make sense. When the world has been turned topsy-turvy or let loose from its moral moorings, chaos and anarchy are enthroned and every moral perversion is justified.

In the ballad "Shoes" an imaginary conversation takes place in the enormous heap of shoes belonging to murdered Jews. They tell the stories of what actually happened to their owners. One of the shoes was worn by a ten year old boy "Whose head was smashed on the wall of the crematorium" because they found him preparing a lesson in Torah.

For a moment all shoes quieted down,
Silence prevailed —
From out of the heap
Burst out a protesting outcry:
How was it that the heavens didn't open?
How come the skies did not break apart?
Hearing the cries and seeing the terror
Of burning children and the slaughter of babes?
How is it conceivable of the Master of the World
Not to have risen from His throne and
Not to have relented from His wrath
And not to have shown mercy to His children?

— Baruch Rotman, "Na'alaim"

Perhaps it is so. Perhaps God does not care. We cannot fully ascertain that. And there are still more questions to be asked. A similar question is being raised by the poet in behalf of the martyrs. Most poets speak in their own behalf. They react, each according to his or her level of personal emotions. Some brandish their fists toward Heaven. Others speak more haltingly and still others couch their venomous sarcasm in the euphemistic terminology of liturgy, an ingenius disguise possible only in the literature of our religious civilization. But who speaks for those whose lives were mercilessly curtailed before they could decide for themselves whether to submit to their fate or rebel against it?

B. Mordecai appears before God, as it were, and addresses Him in behalf of the martyrs:

. . . I came, my Lord, here I am!
I am that wretched Jew
Who under Your skies
Refuses to have anything to do
With Your world.
Actually, for years I have owned nothing
Now I do not even have any tears left.
All my loved ones are here with me
Their outcry concealed in their blood.
The earth will not cover them, so

I brought them to Thee . . .
I don't see their glory
Faded from the faces is their glee
To see them and live, is an impossibility.
And who will be their spokesman
Between You and them?
Many things still untold they can
Tell You, of which You never heard
They went to meet You, this is why
They have reached You here,
They trusted in You
That You would come to meet them.
So I have come to Thee
The cry of my brother is in me,
Whereto can I run away
From his cry?
I came to implore You:
Hearken please to their mute wail.
Had You listened to the last of their
Echo's cry: We want to live!
Had You unlocked the present muteness
Of their plea: Revenge! . . .
An everlasting divide exists between us,
Let them cover heaven's eyes
I have no echo to offer them
Nor a word for a dirge.
I regret all the martyrdom
For Your sake,
Because . . .We served You in vanity . . .

— B. Mordecai, "B'har Ha'elohim"

The echo of the Jewish lament reverberates throughout the Jewish world: "Had You hearkened to our cry . . . How could You be silent . . . You have heard, seen and were not moved . . ." All these anguished outcries undermine our inner tranquility and place us before the eternal abyss of the inexplicable mysterious and esoteric: "I will not respond!" There are unmitigated agonies, psychologically exacerbating, when one's endurance has been pushed beyond imaginable limits. In such times man's ethical propriety disintegrates in the crucible of supreme anguish and despair. Then respectful argument turns into a scathing and scalding reproach: "Be ashamed Lord . . . confess before me . . . offer Your cry before me . . . admit publicly that You art bankrupt . . ." These alarming outbursts of protestations and reprimands make us keenly aware of the spiritual perplexity which has existed since the tragic confrontation with the Holocaust nightmare. This infernal dream has been aptly summarized by the poet who has Rachel bewail the fate of her children and thus thunder out her accusation:

> Why have You unleashed Your fury
> Upon my doves?
> What sort of sin have they committed —
> Disclose it to me — for
> What crime of my darlings
> Led them to be massacred?
> Why, my God, Lord of compassion,
> Have You invoked the rod of Your anger
> To destroy cruelly the fruit of my womb?
> Judge of the world —
> Why have You endowed me with sensory perception
> To feel the quiver of my children . . .
> To smell the smoke of their burned bodies;
> Look at the heap of ashes,
> A bloody heap in the valley of tears . . .
>
> — Zerach Halevi, "Rachel Mevaka Al Baneha"

Our contemporary poets, including the poets of the Holocaust period, often resorted to the most effective method of using the heroes of our people as representatives to present the protest of our people. Abraham and Rachel: Akiba; and even Elisha Ben Avuya, the famous Tanaitic heretic, Rabbi Levi Yitzchak of Berdichov, are used as prototypes sharing their people's tragedy and serving as the spiritual mentors of their communities at the moment of their irreversible annihilation. They spoke up. They made their voices heard whether it was with bitter indignation, or with raising of fists against brutal man or Heaven, or with benign resignation accepting their lot without a murmur or complaint. Be it as it may; their loud protest or silent rebellion did not go down with them to their mass grave or escape through Zyklon B in the gas chambers and evaporate into nothingness. Their human reaction and natural rejection of their lot still shrills in our hearts and their demand for an answer from God still lingers on, and it will remain searching for its "Tikkun" like the forlorn soul in Kabbalistic speculation. In the meantime, the generation of Auschwitz survivors and the rest of mankind must live with this oppressive thought which has turned into a theological, historical, and psychological disturbance of far reaching consequences.

In Y. Sh. Schwartz' "Harav Vehadayan" we hear a shattering protest from the Rabbi whose disciple and colleague is psychologically shocked upon hearing this God-fearing shepherd of his community. The poet exposes before us a frightening picture of the Nazi *Endloesung* action. Part of the community is "selected" to be exterminated and part to be enslaved in torturous Concentration Camps to die a slower death.

Mothers try to pacify their sobbing children
While the rest of the community
Proceeds in a mute anguish
The Elul sun is heating up
And shining . . .

There is still a beautiful world!
(They think to themselves)
How difficult it is to part from it
Even from a hoarse cricket . . .

At the head of the community marches the Rabbi, Reb David Hakohen and at his side the Dayan, Rabbi Noah, his devoted disciple and friend. They have been inextricably bound to each other in their long personal and spiritual relationship. They march "silently like mutes" and this silence is strange, tense and oppressive. At that moment Rabbi Noah turns to his master, looks at him with a broken heart and says:

My master . . .
Is this the way of our end,
Has the end come upon us all?
Have we that much sinned
That the Lord entrapped us
Into an inescapable predicament?
And are we prohibited from questioning
God's behavior?
This is my anguish that speaks out

From my shattered body —
And we remain silent
As the sword is put to our throat?

The Old Rabbi hastens to answer in unmistakable terms:

Rabbi Noah! You have asked me:
"Have we that much sinned . . .?
Look behind you
At the entire community . . .
Is there one known murderer among them?
Count, please, the thieves,
The drunkards who reeled in their vomit,
The ones who destroyed families
For the favors of a prostitute . . .

Are these the offenders and the transgressors
For which Heaven meted out
Its retribution?
And if even Moses and Akiba
And Rabbi Chanina ben Tradyon
Would justify heavenly action
I will not believe it,
I cannot believe it that the
Household of Israel sinned that much
To be torn apart with Samael's nails!
And what about the "Big Talk"?
"The Lord is merciful, long suffering, full
Of kindness and truth . . .
"You are the children of your God" . . .
"For as a father smitest his son
So will the Lord punish you" —
These fancy words fall painfully
On our heart —
With their bitter derision . . .
Had the Father measured the depth
Of our tortures which He inflicted
Upon His wretched sons and daughters:
When they were entangled
In the dark coil of suffering?
Did he look into the heart of a mother
When her treasured infant
Was turned into a lump of flesh

Before her very eyes . . .?
Rabbi Noah! . . .
There is no mercy, no kindness, no clemency,
And justice is trampled and righteousness
is mocked
Both on the earth below and in the heavens above,
And the cup of comfort is nothing but a cup
of venom!
We have erred with our fathers!
There is no justice nor is there a judge!
And he who possess weapons, murders!
And he who has fire burns down,
And there is no one to stop him!
And no lion gives up his prey from between
his teeth!

Rabbi Noah was totally shaken to his innermost recesses upon hearing his righteous master's words of brimstone and fire against Heaven. Shaken, amazed and bewildered he mumbled out his rebuttal: "Is this how Rabbi David is speaking who was once the source of envigorating and inspiring faith?" He was simultaneously angry and pitied his teacher. With great trepidation he turns to his beloved friend and master and says:

My Rabbi, from the day I met you
I loved you!
Woe unto me that I had to see you
In this predicament!

The poem concludes with both sobbing — the master who could no longer restrain his despair and the disciple and colleague whose faith has been seared by the Holocaust conflagration, no matter how pure and chaste their faith may have continued in the God of Israel.

Again, this protest amidst faith, flaunting refutation of God while truly hestitating about its justification, is a Jewish trait. The inner mentality of the Jewish free soul is unencumbered from supposedly inherited original sins. The Jew, the poet, the victim, the spokesman for himself or for the victims or the people — spoke his mind. Whereas in the past he spoke similar words with profuse apologies, this poetry of the last *churban* is totally free of the fetters of remorse or apologetics. It is no longer defensive. It was steeled in the fires of Auschwitz and bathed in the blood of the faithful. Judaism emerged in a kind of maturity unknown heretofore. Hebrew poetry reflected it faithfully.

Thus spoke a pious father to his son:

Why was God silent
And why did He fail to avenge our blood!
God did not pay attention
To our supplication:
O Lord destroy our foe!
Wither the arm of the profane
For decapitating a Jewish mother
Or stabbing her to death with his dagger
Wither the arm of that uncircumcised Gentile
Who buried mother and father alive . . .
Remember my son . . .
Remember that cry . . .
I adjure you to testify
To every transport of Jews
Doomed to die
In crematorium!
My son
You live
In the generation
Of Jewish extermination . . .

— Israel Erlich, "Al Hadam"

These bitter, hard-hitting words have served as a salutary psychological ventilation. Without this opportunity for rebelliousness, the religious recuperation from the Holocaust trauma would have been crippled. We must beware, however, of confusing tradition with theology. Paradoxically enough, we prayed, we observed Pesach, Yom Kippur . . . we remembered. Tradition was continued in Auschwitz.

Moreover, tradition has validated its essential importance as the unifying force of our people everywhere and for always. Theology has been forced to undergo a fundamental change in its attitude because of the Auschwitz experience. We may use the same linguistic categories and postulates but their interpretations and meaning have undergone metamorphases in order to conform to the ontology of the Holocaust event. Post-Holocaust theology, therefore, became subject to an imperative revision in order to make any sense. The complexity of theological speculation has been for too long detached from a reality that dissolves the very spiritual ground from under our feet. Consequently, the need to follow the law of parsimony is essential. Theology, to become intelligible, must make sense. Man today begins as a skeptic. He wants first to know before he can believe. No argument to the contrary will change these contemporary facts after Auschwitz. Honest faith need not be complex. Auschwitz has shaken theological anachronisms from their roots and a revamping of thinking is of crying necessity to enable man to regain his rudimentary faith in a theocentered universe, whose ethics may restore the faith in man as well.

Thus the poetic expressions which we have quoted until now, have in their own simple and non-theological terminology reflected the problems Auschwitz created for us in its aftermath.

Within these theological protestations we find pious obsequiousness, words seemingly spoken with humility and trepidation but under whose guise sharp inveighing against Heaven can be discovered.

> I lost my way to You
> Your face is seen no more
> Bloody clouds have arisen between us
> I am lost in the darkness.
> Yesterday I hid my face in Your bosom
> And You appeared to listen with compassion
> To the voice of Your son,
> Today from the shadows
> Have I emerged before You.
> I submitted the purity
> Of my youthful dream
> As a gift unto You.
> From every dark ambush
> The robber is lurking.
> The Creator of Light
> Brighten my way to behold You
> I am so lonely and forsaken in Your forest
> Will You stand aloof while my life is at stake?
> Where are You Lord? Where are You?

— Tanchum Berman, "Ayeka"

If the above quoted poem is perceivable within the context of the author's predicament, the subsequent verses demonstrate an inbred piety too strong to allow protest against God even while life was ebbing in the shadow of the Nazi gallows . . .

> I am afraid to complain
> Lest I may curse You
> And invoke Your ire
> Not only through the German,
> Not only through the nations
> Who sought my life
> And rejoiced over my demise . . .
> I am afraid lest I curse,
> And blaspheme my Lord
> Also You . . .
> And I will become dumbfounded
> My Lord . . .
>
> — Ari Even-Zahav, "Nochach Hash'mad"

Above all else, the very source of the Jew's litigation with God is rooted primarily in the psychological aspect of the partnership which the Jew entered with God at the moment of his national birth. This covenant was spelled out in a mutually binding partnership between God and Abraham. Within this framework of reference it is no wonder that the Jew felt at home with God and carried on his millenial dialogue with Him as a matter of course.

History, in Judaism, does not refer to historical facts alone. We understand our history as the story of our chosen existence where facts reflect God's guiding hand in the evolving story of our particular existence. Hence, the biography of our people contains the mixture of faith and fact, destiny and consequence, religion and civilization, culture and Torah, ethical precepts and universal law, God and Israel, God's theophany and His obscondity (hiddenness), independence and Exile, Holocaust and the State of Israel. It is an unending evolutionary process, inexplicable, fascinating, frustrating, haunting with its mystery of an ever-dying, ever-living eternal Israel.

The "covenant" that God made with Abraham enabled us also to have an equal right to challenge each other's fidelity in upholding its terms. Just as God can take Israel to task for its failure to live up to the tenets of the agreement, so can Israel sue God for His seeming failure to uphold the terms of the covenant. There is general agreement that this fateful covenant made at the birth of our Jewish peoplehood, has cemented and united our people no matter how dispersed; has shaped our national and religious ideas and ideals, and has given meaning to our special relationship with God throughout the generations.

Not all poets, however, have embraced the covenant as their rallying point for triumphant odes. On the contrary, upon reflection some of them looked upon this cherished covenant as an onerous burden. For if the covenant is our protecting shield and insurance against the predators of history, it has been found to serve as a pacifier rather than a shield. For if the covenant spelled out the special mission of Israel, why did we suffer so much and were so often decimated by the enemies of God? "Is this the recompense for Torah?" became the theme of the rabbinic outcry . . .

The poet Yitzchak Lamdan, in his book *B'ma'aleh Akrabim* (On The Hill of Scorpions), aims his entire argument against the covenant. According to him, this covenant has chained us to our bitter destiny from which we cannot extricate ourselves. Our people, he claims, have been tied to an esoteric mission which we have not been able to change or refute.

> From our very ancient beginning,
> At the dawn of our nation's birth,
> Our Father has envisioned
> In the covenant "Between the Pieces"
> The terrible trinity:
> God — Israel — Vulture.
> How frightened was Abraham's heart
> And woe, how fearful and trembling he was
> When he saw the preying bird
> Hovering over the cadavers of the future . . .
>
> And upon which cut-up pieces
> Wilt Thou my Lord
> Descend in distant times?

This is how Abraham posed his question in deep perplexity when he beheld the shocking sight. The fateful reply did not tarry:

> Return to your pieces, Abraham!
> Always to your pieces, return!

Wherever your sacrifice will be bound
For whomever you will yearn
The black wing will replace
The terrifying shadow —

I will always reveal Myself to you
At night and in the gloom of darkness.

The Jewish people have been always caught in the pincers of its fate, saturated with innocent blood, and immersed in insufferable pain. With no succor or relief in sight, the covenant becomes a burdensome yoke to carry, but it is placed upon us arbitrarily:

And is this the covenant with me?
Is that all of it?
This is the covenant Abram!
Arise, go forth and carry its yoke!

Lamdan continues to bemoan his people's being sacrificed "upon the eternal gallows" and its wrestling with its fatal lot. He makes Jacob, his protagonist, lodge his sorrowful complaint:

God's trap
Is hidden from me
And the ambush
Is limitless.

He tries to break away from his destiny and he thanks God through Jacob, his chosen beloved, but also the most despised among men:

No! Thank You! I don't want anymore
To come, to listen
And be again beloved by God
And scorned by man!

Jacob struggles with all his might to liberate himself from the special position God gave him, as if saying with Rashi: "I want neither your honey nor your sting." Jacob rejects God's invitation to renew the confidential relationship even though it is a distinct honor:

I do not want Your love
Or its pain . . .

In Your treasure house of love
There is not to be found
One crumb of kindness
Nor a ray of light . . .

And under the weight of its faith
I have sunk to the ground!
If this is love
Leave me rather, my intimate friend!
Leave me alone,
And let me join the community
Of insignificant people in the world . . .

Jacob continues his quarrel with God and denounces Israel's election and its results:

You had me uprooted
From the heart of the world,

That I might belong to Thee alone
And be with Thee alone[15]

Lamdan draws upon the midrashic source of Jacob's vision of his rebellion,[16] elaborating his own version in which Jacob endearvors to cut off all the strings that tie him to his destiny. The elected one seems to be chosen for slaughter and massacre. Jacob wants to escape from this strange prison of love. For too long, and for too many generations, has Israel suffered torture for the sake of this divine love affair:

Leave me alone! I don't want
To be dragged in again
Against my own free will
To the scaffold of Your love
My lover and seducer!

Do not come again to persuade me, Jacob warns. Do not call upon me again:

Leave me alone . . .
I do not want to come again,
I do not want to hear again!

Uri Tzi Greenberg actually summarized the complaint motif in the Holocaust poetry by pointing to its rootedness in the wellsprings of faith as expressed so intrepidly in this poem of Rabbi Levi Yitzchak of Berdichov:

> Either, or, Master of the Universe!
> You are not accustomed
> To have a Jew rise up
> And challenge You.
> You are used to hearing his adorations
> His cantorial melodies.
> You are accustomed to see Him
> Pour his heart out in tears
> With drops of blood, with torn heart,
> With tottering knees
> On a fast day —
> But now the wheel won't move my Lord!
> I won't let it,
> Not at all!
> Either, or!
> I Levi Yitzchak of Berdichev,
> Demand Your exalted reply!

5. Protest Against God's Hiding His Face (Deus Obsconditus)

> And the children of my people
> Who have been chosen forever,
> The voice of the slaughtered for generations
> Rise from the depths of the earth,
> Once again have they been "chosen" to be sacrificed
> And the Lord is silent and
> Hides behind the scenes.

— Kalman Bartini, "Shir V'heydo"

The possibility of God's-hiding-His-face, or God's silence has been one of the classical answers in theology and has been reintroduced in view of God's supposed silence during the Holocaust. The subject had already been broached by the prophets. The prophet Jeremiah implores God on behalf of the people to instruct them what to do. The land was besieged, the people in mortal danger. But . . . "After ten days, the word of the Lord came to

Jeremiah." (*Jeremiah* 42:2) In *Ezekiel,* we find the following reference: "O mortal, speak to the elders of Israel and say to them: Thus saith the Lord God: Have you come to inquire of me? As I live, I will not respond to your inquiry, declares the Lord God." (*Ezekiel* 20:1) Here we have strong indications of God's hiding-His-face . . . an aspect much discussed and little understood, the easiest solution to God's silence, but also the most contested and most vulnerable to attack.

Rabbi Nachman of Bratzlav proposed a novel interpretation of "Hester Panim," of God's hiding-His-face. He claims, with Kabbalistic fervor, that God by necessity must remove Himself from the world and create a *Chalal Hapanui,* a void. Since nothing can be outside God, God's uninterrupted omnipresence prevents the existence of reality. Once He effects His absence, He enables reality to enter into man's world, thus setting the stage for man to act on his own free accord . . . this is indeed an ingenious suggestion. But herein lies the lugubrious fact that man when left to his own free will, can scale the heights of sainthood and simultaneously descend to the abyss of bestiality.

The psalmist of old summarized the issue in one verse:

> Why O Lord has Thou neglected me
> And hid Thy countenance from me?
>
> — *Psalms* 85:15

In Holocaust poetry and in post-Holocaust theology, it received thorough scrutiny. The issue is based upon the postulate that God shares with man a common purpose to perfect the world and there is, by necessity, a mutual dependence in the theological sense.[17]

Martin Buber defines the condition of divine obscondity as "the eclipse of God." Emil Fackenheim[18] explains this phenomenon in terms of lunar and solar eclipses. As these eclipses are temporary by their very nature, so are we to perceive the times of God's hiddeness as temporary in nature. He is the only one who determines the time of His self-imposed hiding and the time for His re-emergence.

Shlomo Tana reminds us of the miraculous rescue of Chananiah, Mishael and Azariah from the burning furnace, and he fulminates with rage as to why we in the crematoria should not have deserved the same miracle:

Nowadays, bereft of lore and legend
So many have been thrown into the burning pit,
Their bodies were consumed, only ashes remained,
Not even one was saved.
No angel did come.
How great was the betrayal.
And every time we tried to escape or obstruct,
The fumes of fires would kill us at once,
And God's way remains a riddle.

— "Reyach Ha'esh"

The riddle of this *Mysterium Tremendum* is part of God's hiding, silence or absence, and part of the nagging inquiry: "Where art Thou, O Lord?"

In his study on the question of God's silence in the Bible and Auschwitz, Prof. Andre Neher[19] mentions Elie Weisel's observation, that from the days of Auschwitz one can no longer view the story of "Isaac's binding" as an imaginary tale. In Auschwitz it was the definitive and irreversible reality. In addition, were Abraham and Isaac to appear before the inmates of Auschwitz bleeding from torture and in agony, they would surely grab us by our throats and instead of asking: "Where is the sheep for a substitute?" they would certainly ask "Where is God?"

Neither in the Bible nor in theology that followed later, do we find a plausible explanation of this mystery except the one of Rabbi Nachman mentioned above. The prophet Isaiah put it succinctly: "My thoughts are not your thoughts, and your ways are not mine saith the Lord." (Chp. 55) The poet Hameiri puts it:

We will never understand You
Nor what You do . . .

— "Hamoked Haran"

The stance of resignation, never to know God's ways and plans, was acceptable for countless generations. The Holocaust Apocalypse removed pious patience and religious equanimity from Jews. Meir Bossak expresses the new impatience without reservation:

For man will not see Me and live?

And yet we have seen His countenance
Amen, I know . . .

I know, the day will come
The poets will come
And sing odes to God.
But they
Will never know
That they have seen only
One of His thousands of robes
His shadow they felt —
His back
The mask on His face (at most)
They have seen . . .
But we, we beheld His face
The countenance of God
The burning flame in His eyes
We have seen Him
Hovering in eternity
Destroying and rebuilding worlds
In the darkness of infinity and void
His hands like lightning-revolutions
Kneading out the future,
Like the baker kneads the dough
Before he gives shape to bread.
We saw His building hands
And His hard fingers we felt,
As parts of our bodies were excised
When blood was dripping from our wounds
As He was exposing every nerve
When the skin was torn off from what was
Left of our bodies.
We have seen You, God,
Building and destroying worlds
You awesome and terrible,
We have seen You, Lord . . .

Indeed, we the witnesses of the Holocaust contend that the essence of "The Mystery" has been revealed to us in all its terrifying nature:

The convenant — in its frightening darkness; the binding of Isaac — its trauma we felt in our flesh;

God's hiding face — we experienced in the Ghettos, Concentration Camps, crematoria, and common graves . . .

Well then, should this be categorized as heresy, blasphemy, sarcasm or be dismissed as sophomoric thinking? Should we rather accept trite, archaic, theological prescriptions, and continue in our soporific state of interpretations which evade the truth? Of course, we will agree that there is a need for a new definition. But before we find this desired definition, let us see first what is being said with *ex-cathedra* seriousness pertaining to God's place in the Holocaust . . .

God is with the suffering, His voice is heard in the anguish of the tortured . . . God is present wherever and whenever man is persecuted, hounded, enslaved, harried and exploited . . . God is found in the tragic predicament when man dangles between life and death. God is found in the agony of man, in his despair and forlorness. God manifests His presence especially where man, in the clutches of death and torture, perserves in kindness and humanness and discovers, as Viktor Frankl did, that concern and love can be shared, and new meaning given to life even moments before death. Thus God's voice is heard through man's response to sanctify life. In the will to live, in spite of pernicious evil, man reassures the future and thus testifies to man's responsiveness to God's call . . . and thus fulfills the behest of Fackenheim's "Eleventh Commandment": "Thou shalt not give Hitler a posthumous victory."

Some will offer the proposition to consider the Holocaust in the larger context of our tear-filled Jewish experiences of death, persecution and suffering, with only the statistical dimension making the case of the Holocaust different.

Others say: The Holocaust is a tragedy. It is man's responsibility and duty to confront evil in the world and combat it to make sure that evil will not be triumphant in the world again. Or we encounter this sanctimonious entry: Experience teaches that suffering may turn out to be a blessing in disguise . . . (The apparent application of the rabbinic dictum: "There's no evil which does not turn out for the good" to the cataclysm of the Holocaust, shows a total lack of understanding of the enormity of our tragedy. To argue that we should see God as preserving the other two-thirds of our people, rather than protesting the murder of one-third, is nothing but an insult to those who were martyred and no less to the survivors. It is sheer myopic insensitive piety. What would this theologian have told us had Hitler succeeded in perfecting an atomic weapon first, then killing two-thirds of our people? Would he have sung Halleluiah to God for His miraculous saving of one-third?)

And finally, there are others with the audacity to suggest that the price of "six million" martyrs was paid for reestablishing the Jewish State. What a horrendous thought! . . . What Zionist would dare to accept such a bloody exchange?

As we can see, there has been a sincere, oft times naive and painful attempt to confront the reality of Auschwitz and give it some theological meaning. But *in toto* the theologians have failed to grapple with the impossible dimensions of the Holocaust event. Some have tried hard while others have speculated with nonsense. Much verbiage, many cliches, many worn-out theological slogans have been pronounced but none have touched the heart of the Holocaust tragedy. Most of those involved in this speculation did not experience the existential nature of Auschwitz. With the best of intentions the profundity of the *Shoah* is incomprehensible. Frankly, those who venture into theological speculation in view of Auschwitz, must pose to themselves this question: What would have been my reaction, my thoughts, my response to the ultimate question were I in the gas chamber? What has my brother thought at the moment when he was confronted with his death and all his ardent faith and ideals have not borne out his expectations as a Jew? For good measure, they might ask these additional questions: For whom should the theologians speak? For the six million? For the surviving witnesses? Or only for those who were not there?

The Holocaust is an object lesson which compels us to continue "in spite of it" and be part of the world we live in. Its implications and the dynamics of the heroic and spiritual resistance of the victims are of incalculable importance for the Jewish future and Israel's existence. Our post-Holocaust resilience, in spite of our decimation, is legendary. It has been our superhuman active response to ring a death knell to our despair at the moment of realization of the dimensions of our tragedy. The hour of our liberation was also the commencement of our physical, psychological and spiritual restoration, from out of the ashes of Nazi annihilation. We reaffirmed our commitment to *Kiddush Hachaim,* to reassert, rededicate and resanctify our life, instead of dedicating our life to the morose prospect of becoming *Aveyley-Hashoah* the perennial mourners of the Holocaust and glorifiers of *Kiddush-Hashem,* of martyrdom. We went over to the offensive, that is to say: we had enough martyrdom and enough martyrs to last us for an eternity. We had enough lamentations, threnodies, *yahrtzeits* and memorial days of fasting, mourning and memorialization . . . We suffered alone and we must rely on ourselves alone once again to live for the sake of those who died and for the sake of our posterity and people!

(We were alone in our tragedy and we were alone in our survival, no army, no war effort, no sacrifices were made by any of the Allied forces to hasten the saving of our lives. If and when we were liberated, it was accidentally and of secondary importance. Not one soldier seems to have died in trying to save us. Had there been this moral consideration as part of the military strategy, many could have been saved. It is Elie Wiesel who called to our attention the sad fact that after the war we were not treated as humanity's victims for whose benefit all technical and legal laws and rules should have been suspended, as a gesture of empathy and remorse for having let it happen.)[20]

(We the victims became "displaced persons" in refugee camps and all the rigors of law were applied to us when we applied for immigration visas to the United States and other countries in the free world. We, the emaciated broken reeds, were kept waiting for years until entrance visas were granted. We often had to undergo degrading medical examinations, and interrogations to prove that we were sound of mind and physically fit. Thus, those whom Hitler broke in mind and body became the "rejects" and undesirables Only the poor, beleagured, struggling Israel embraced her sons and daughters and granted a home to the homeless victims of the Holocaust. The leaders of the free world, beset by narrow self interest and prejudices, continued to make a mockery of moral responsibility and ethical sensibility.)

The persistent Jobian question has not been answered, nor can the mystery of the Holocaust ever be answered. The Holocaust is a mystery, for want of a better term. *The Holocaust is not a historical event, a chapter in the history of World War II.* The Holocaust and its dimensions cannot be relegated and analyzed in the light of historical dialectics alone. Historical facts are not enough, just as God's absence in Auschwitz is not the sole reason for our destruction. Just as there is danger in theologizing the *Shoah,* so there lurks a still greater danger in leaving the Holocaust in the hands of fact-finding technicians. Much too often we encounter historians who play the role of psychoanalysts of events, who select facts and subject them to misinterpretation and misrepresentation. We need perspective in order to digest and perceive the enormity of the Holocaust catastrophe.

Some theologians, for example, are too narcissistic, embracing their own coinage of theological slogans and in the end they lose sight of the Holocaust and its consequences. Revisionist historians have already embarked upon the de-demonization of Nazism and are rewriting, with pernicious perversion, the facts of the Holocaust nightmare. Thus they proceed to invalidate the "over-emotionalism" of Jewish historians. Neo-Nazis support attempts to spray the world with outright lies, by rewriting history. Communist historians rewrite the history of the Holocaust in terms of Fascism as a product of the decadent West and forget conveniently that the prime targets and the greatest sufferers were the Jews. They include Jews within the national groups who were victimized without identifying the Jew as a Jew. The Jew seems to reappear intermittently in his national uniqueness and his name resurrected with derision only when needed for political, ideological, and anti-Semitic target practice.

In a synoptic review on the theological aspects of the Holocaust, Prof. Eliezer Berkovitz has most adroitly succeeded in exposing the issue with the flair of an objective thinker and with the fervor of an intellectual, sensitive religious Jew.[21] His sincere respect for "Holy Disbelief" which he interprets to mean the loss of faith in Auschwitz, is to him as valid as the faith of those who died in their submission to the "Will of God." To accept faith, he contends, as "one who was not there myself" is to challenge their rejection without knowing what it meant to be there and lose one's faith. "I am not Job, I am only his brother." On the other hand, to reject and rebel is also impossible because this would mean the "desecration of the sacrifice of the myriads who accepted their lot in faith." "How dare I reject if they accepted?" The rabbinic dictum is aptly applicable in this holy predicament: "Oy Li Me'Yotzri, V'oy Li Me'Yitzri" in essence, I am in trouble by rejecting or affirming . . . This twilight zone of mind staggering dilema can be very oppressive. Thus Berkowitz concludes:

> In the presence of the holy faith of the crematoria, the ready-faith of those who were not there is vulgarity. But the disbelief of the sophisticated intellectual in the midst of an affluent society — in the light — of the holy disbelief of the crematoria — that is obscenity . . .

> We must believe because our brother Job believed; and we must question because our brother Job so often could not believe any more. This is not a comfortable situation; but it is our condition in this era after the Holocaust.

In short, the intrinsic flaw in all the theological arguments pertaining to the Holocaust is the honest attempt to "explain away" casuistically, some more ingeniously than others, the "problem" rather than to confront it head-on.

Theologically, God's divine power embraces the whole of the universe as Isaiah stated:

> I am the Lord and there is none except me . . .
> I form light and create darkness . . .
> I make peace and create evil
> I the Lord do all these things . . .
>
> — *Isaiah,* Chp. 45

If this be the case, we must declare ourselves totally incapable of defining God and His role in the Holocasut. It would have been more courageous and worthy of our theologians to do this than to pose as the proverbial wrestlers with God and second guess Him as to what He meant to do, did, or will yet do. The medieval Jewish philosopher Joseph Albo declared: "Ilu Yedativ, Heyitiv" (If I were to "know" God (His nature) I would be God).[22] To reinterpret God's attributes, which have been man's own invention to begin with, in order to make them fit someone's theory of God's place in the Holocaust Apoclypse is to run the risk of arriving at ridiculous conclusions. The most striking example is the case of declaring God innocent of creating evil. (This matter has never set well with our theologians anyway.) Therefore, to render God free of any guilt of evil in the world, the theologians presented Him as an innocuous ethical deity, who is suffering from man's perfidy against man, but must defer intervention in man's affairs in order not to violate man's rights as a free agent, lest He inhibit man's freedom of choice. Hence, the merciful Lord, who makes for absolute goodness, speaks with great sorrow and empathy through the larynx of every human who suffers unjustly. Another of these genial theological suggestions makes rational sense but it is hard to swallow: God's patience and power is demonstrated in the fact of God's own self-imposed control, like hiding His face, when

He deems it necessary. Go and dare to tell this to that tragic victim of the *Sonder-Kommando* who left a note in which he said

> I wonder whether one day I shall be able to cry again . . .

Such theologizing opens a Pandora's box of surging questions one more scathing than the other, *ad infinitum.*

In all honesty, these are perhaps useful and soothing answers and reassuring theologies for those who dare not recall the original question. But, for a generation that was in the Nazi inferno, and for those who returned from there, such theologizing is of no value.

Yitzchak Ivri addresses the issue head-on:

> My faith has evaporated
> In You, and in Your
> Heavenly administration . . .
> Look: the entire world
> Goes up in fire
> And drowns in blood . . .
>
> I just don't care
> For fancy pronouncements
> I want real action from You!
> Disclose to me a new secret
> Inaugurate a new set of commandments
> And inscribe them on a tablet!
>
> Then command these rules upon me . . .
> For this was the pristine reason
> For Your creating me
> To obey and fulfill them!
> And if You are the commander
> And if You desire my fidelity
> Then augment Thy own power
> And rule over Satan . . .!
>
> — *Beyn Dam L'dam*

Our sages in the Talmud (*T.B. Yoma* 69b) have addressed this issue with much greater courage than today's sophisticated theologians. The discussion ensued as to why both Jeremiah and Daniel tampered with the original text of Moses' invocation of the

Lord's attributes: "Hael Hagadol, Hagibor Vehanora" (*Deut.* 10:17) (The Great, The Mighty and The Awesome God . . .)

Jeremiah who witnessed the destruction of the First Temple, addressed God: "O great and mighty God" (*Jer.* 32:18), leaving out "awesome." Daniel who saw the enslavement of his brethren after the destruction, addressed God: "O great and awesome God" (*Daniel* 9:4), leaving out "mighty." The sages inquired: "Heychi Ovdi V'kori Takanta D'takin Moshe?" (How could Jeremiah and Daniel tamper with (or abolish) the text established by Moses!) And Rabbi Eliezer gave the answer: Since they have experienced great traumatic and agonizing events and they well know that God insists upon the truth, "Lefichach Lo Kizvu Bo" (Therefore they would not ascribe to God false attributes). That is to say, that since they could not address God with all the praises of His mercy and kindness in view of what they saw, they skipped these attributes, because they did not feel like invoking them. These attributes did not conform or correspond to the reality of events and so they omitted them. Thus, says Rabbi Eliezer, there is no reason to be angry at people for being honest about their feelings.

This is the most important didactic lesson for all those who venture into the field of post-Holocaust theology, an area completely different from normal theology. In view of the Holocaust, God's will and God's ways defy any attempt to discuss this matter in the once accepted manner of theological discourse. The Holocaust is beyond explanation. Thus the poet offers some insight in his moments of poetic vision; the *Ba'al-Midrash-Hashoah,* Elie Wiesel offers a tale in which he formulates his specific questions. The historian at best unravels documents, discovers new evidence, establishes the chronology of events and dates, but the theologian remains "holding-the-bag". It is a formidable task to face. How can we, out of the ashes of Auschwitz, rescue some living sparks to give meaning to our existence, confidence in our future and succor to our mourners? The poets and other writers in the Ghettos and Concentration Camps rendered an invaluable service. They sang the songs of our Third-*Churban* and of its aftermath. They served as the front-line soldiers who courageously refused to yield. They knew of no retreat. They confronted the issue and proved combat ready with holy-disbelief, for their faith was terribly charred by the flames of the crematoria.

To be sure, there are no answers as to why the *Shoah* took place nor is there an explanation good enough to take theodicy seriously.

For this reason, the generation after Auschwitz and the generations that follow will continue sinking in a theological quagmire. There is such a thing as accepting reality and another of inquiring into divine logic. The reality of Auschwitz is so horrifying that it defies rationality. Divine logic is so far beyond man's comprehension that it must be left to its own fate.

Man in the twilight zone must, however, make some sense out of Auschwitz, survival, rebirth, continuation. We must keep on with the search while retaining our faith.

From the poetry on hand, we can safely conclude that poetry did not go to extremes. It posed the ultimate questions succienctly, it reflected ultimate concerns. It dared to speak intrepidly, and unflinchingly voiced its protest. Yet it did not exhaust in its rational rhetoric all the logical possibilities which might have driven it into either extreme: total heresy or total submission.

If this is the case, if the poetry with its celebrated license stopped short of these extremes, what telling value did it have? What accomplishments are there in leaving us suspended? Yaakov Cahan seems to offer an indirect answer to our question in his drama: *Acher.* In one of the scenes Elisha Ben Avuyah expresses his view that in spite of the reality of God, His providential powers do not exist. After due and exhaustive contemplation, Elisha does not hesitate to go to the very bitter end of his rational argument. The truth to him is above any other consideration. But in spite of the clarity of his logic, an undercurrent of subtle doubt can be detected. The problem is: Is logical truth all that absolute?[23]

If we are to resort to rational decisions exclusively, we run the risk, very often, of losing the last spark of hope. Can we afford, in all honesty, to pursue this road? If we assume that there is still some hope left, and it is forbidden to despair of our existence, how then can we confront the abysses of life without a spark of genuine faith? How can a scourged remnant, from the ashes of Auschwitz, restore itself to a new life while accepting Elisha's rational conclusion: "There is no judgment and no judge" . . .? Perhaps this was Rabbi Meir's question to Elisha his teacher, whose logic transformed him into a frustrated heretic:

> And how do you continue living,
> And how do you bear the suffering
> Of the times, my master?

> Tell me, my master,
> It is a long time since you have prayed!

And Elisha replies:

> To pray — To whom?
> To a hiding God
> Who created the world
> And left it to its own travail
> And to the deceptions of its spirit?

This heretic or agnostic Elisha, who challenged the theologies and theodicies of others, shows, at the end of his rational defense, the beginnings of doubts in his own logic. He begins to be uncertain whether there is anything more concrete, valid and convincing in his ideas than in the ideas of the rest of the sages of Israel who remained faithful to their religious heritage.

Here is one of the classical sensitive souls who, by the standards of those ancient days, "went astray" after his intellectual conclusion that all life is vanity and absurdity. Because of this supposed logic, he destroyed himself. Hence, neither logic nor faith provide the answer to the Holocaust catastrophe. They contain nebulous clues, which may in time be deciphered.

This perennial struggle between faith and logic remains the dominant undercurrent of the poetry of the Holocaust. Parallel to this battle between the heart and mind runs the argument that it is not as important to expose God's supposed failure as to fathom the depths of the indestructibility of Judaism and the Jewish people, a truth about our destiny that defies all laws of history.

In conclusion, the hard-hitting questions poetry so superbly and intrepidly posed were not aimed at exposing the Achilles' heel of theology's and theodicy's untenable position vis-a-vis the tangible and tragic evidence that the Holocaust presented in its cruelest form. What poetry achieved was not necessarily to accentuate the prevailing difficulties in confronting and contending with the Holocaust within the realm of faith. What it achieved was to dispell the pious naivete of the past. Auschwitz laid to rest naivete and fear. Auschwitz encouraged man to speak his mind. It was the license of the heretic to thunder, to be the celebrated iconoclast, to question, to challenge, and to denounce. Auschwitz opened the mouth of the devout servant, faithful maid, innocent child, to ask, to complain, to demand, to understand why man must suffer. Physical pain and torture have their own immediate destructive effects. But spiritual and mental anguish have devastating and far-reaching results. If life can have meaning, so can suffering if man could only know the reason for it all . . .

The Holocaust's cataclysmic and total destruction for no justifiable reason has eliminated pious submission and self scrupulous accusation. The holy silence of submissive man was broken. Man's humility remained. But man's humbleness in front of the tribunal of justice, before the Judge of all mankind, disappeared. For this reason we find in poetry "straight talk" direct and honest. The refusal to cry in private and pretend in public that all is right had a salutary effect upon the survival of Judaism's faith, and the faith of the victims and survivors.

In all this great and exasperating dialogue, the evidence of a living *corpus* of Judaism was proven. The pulse of our faith has never slowed down. From within the "storm and stress" of the Holocaust experience, notwithstanding holy disbelief or unholy belief, the voice of the authentic Jewish moral conscience was heard loud and clear. The faith of God, in love, in justice and in truth was steeled in the fires of the crematoria. This indestructability of the Jew and his faith was proven not because of Auschwitz, but in spite of Auschwitz . . . Thus the living sparks of our inextinguishable faith in our national destiny has spelled out our hope and faith in the future. As much as the Jew in Auschwitz proclaimed intrepidly and defiantly "*Shma Israel*" so did my ears hear the *Hatikvah* hymn incessantly repeated . . . *He who did not hear the "Shma"* pronounced at the gallows or on the last trip of the mussulmen-inmates to the gas chambers in Birkenau after the infamous Mengele "Selections" in Auschwitz, will never understand the meaning of sanctifying God's name in the name of Israel. And he who did not hear the singing of *Hatikvah* in Auschwitz, will never understand the undying hope of a dying poeple that secured the eternity of Israel, and the miraculous restoration of our people in the Land of our Fathers.

Thus, as long as there is a sensitive conscience, truth will continue to exist. As long as the Jewish heart beats with the rhythm of its ethical heritage, there will be meaning to our life and even suffering will make sense. Not because we want it so to be, as the existentialist Albert Camus would say, but because we have a greater reason and a very long contract with God to live and to witness. We are harnessed to a higher reason which is unfathomable and rationally ineffable but deeply felt in the Jewish soul. Nietzsche was correct when he said: "He who has a why to live for can bear almost any how." The Jewish eternal "Why" was the eternal echo of the "still small voice" which accompanied us in life and death, in the Ghetto and in the gas chamber, which even the pernicious Nazi factories of death were unable to silence . . . This is why our people died with super-human dignity and this is why we survived the Nazi predators and their partners without staining the divine image in us. The same is not true for the rest of the world. For as long as those directly and indirectly responsible for having produced our murderers have not addressed themselves as to "Why" they produced such wicked elements, their divine image will continue to be dimmed no matter how many pious gestures they make. Unless they can find the answer, their guilt will remain inexpiable.

The *Shoah,* to be sure, did not succeed in erradicating the divine in the Jew, and this is why our "complaint against heaven" is the star witness of our affirmation of life, of faith and of God.

This is the prism through which our Jewish complaint against God and its themes will continue to be refracted in contemporary thought. For the last word on this subject we must wait for a long time, perhaps an eternity . . .

NOTES

1. According to Babylonian Talmud (*Berachot,* 77).

2."No man even raises a finger unless it is so proclaimed beforehand from heaven" (*B.T. Chulin,* 97).

3. According to Baruch Spinoza, man has only moral freedom, no control over his physiological needs. He is subject to the laws of nature.

4. The Declaration in *Isaiah* (45:7) "I form light and create darkness . . . I make peace and create woe . . . I am the Lord who does all these things," is in conformity with normative Judaism. In the Torah we find no such ideas. This is a later idea which came into Judaism during the Babylonian exile under the influence of Zoroastrianism. According to deductive thinking, if God is the creator of everything, then evil is also His creation. This is the weakest point in the eternal debate on this subject. The most popular interpretation is: A) God is the creator of good and evil; B) God created a good world. And man created evil; C) Evil is the absence of the good in the world, and man can if he so wills, eradicate evil. The poet Israel Efors relates the source of "All Evils" to God's fatal mistake, for

having failed to prevent man from eating from the "Tree of Knowledge" (the science of destruction).

5. Elie Wiesel, *The Gates of the Forest,* p. 42.

6. *Journal of Ecumenical Studies,* Vol. 14, No. 4 (Fall, 1977), p. 75 [643].

7. See: *Sefer Gzeirot Ashkenz Vetzrfat,* ed. A. M. Haberman. The book covers events from the 10th through the 13th Centuries.

8. *Midrash Mechilta,* D'Rabbi Ishmael, on "B'shalach."

9. "For my thoughts are not your thoughts and your ways are not mine, says the Lord" (*Isaiah* 54).

10. Elie Wiesel, *The Town Beyond the Wall;* Byron L. Sherwin, "Elie Wiesel and Jewish Theology," *Judaism* XVIII, Winter 1969.

11. See a fine referential synopsis of rabbinic sources pertaining to the apparent difficulties of understanding God's absence of justice — *Everyman's Talmud,* by A. Cohen. Also see *A Rabbinic Anthology* by Montefiore and Loewe; *Rabbinic Wisdom and Jewish Values* by Wm. B. Silverman; and *Encyclopedia Judaica.*

12. God, the Talmud tells us, posed in Talit *(R.H.* 17b) and Tefillin (*Ber.* 6N) to demonstrate to Moses the posture of prayer let alone the meaning of prayer to be so great that God himself is supposed to pray . . . (To whom does God pray? To Himself . . . [Chag. 5b])

13. *The War Against the Jews,* Lucy S. Dawidowicz, pp. 136-139.
The Final Solution, Gerald Reitlinger, pp. 95-99.
The Holocaust, Nora Levin, pp. 294-297.

14. Dr. Noach H. Rosenblum in "Hateguvrot L'hastarat Panim B'shirat Hashoah," p. 387, projects this complaint. He bases his argument on one remark made by Uri Tzvi Greenberg: "A generation concerned with its stomach, which does not pray to heaven nor does it concern itself with the question of revenge." The source is too weak for serious attention. Greenberg himself cannot be catagorized if one views him from the background of his poetry. He is also subject to different interpretations . . .

15. Compare this complaint with Meir Mohar's answer in his poem: "Am Nivchar" (*Hapoel Hatzair* XXI, Vol. 21).

The Lord will not ask the opinion of his elected
Whether they want to be chosen . . .
He showers upon us afflictions
Plenty of fear and kindness
Impossible to contain . . .
In vain do they collapse under its burden
In vain do they bemoan each other's life:
Restrain O Lord Thy goodness!
Remove from me all Your kindnesses . . .
I am weary from bearing the weight
Of the election wreath . . .
I cannot . . .
I do not want to carry it anymore . . .

16. Lamdan based Jacob's complaint upon the midrashic comment on *Genesis* 28:11 "The sun set — the sun was extinguished, to teach us, that God caused the sun to set before its diurnal time because he wanted to converse with Jacob in privacy.

This resembles the king who had a secret lover, whom he visited intermittently. Said the king to his servants, "put out the lights and the lanterns because I want to converse with my lover in privacy."

17. Abraham Heschel based his theological opinions on similar propositions.

18. Emil Fackenheim, "About the Divine Eclipse," *Commentary,* (June 1964).

19. Andre Neher, Speech and Silence in Prophecy.

20. One needs only remember the perfidious response of Secretary of State Hall who in the heat of Nazi extermination, on February 25, 1943, in reply to mounting pressure to do something to save Jewish lives, spoke of the defunct Evian Conference of 1938 which ended with unwillingness to find refuge for the Jews fleeing from the Nazis, and concluded that the United States would be bound by its immigration laws. He went on to emphasize that the problem was not uniquely Jewish adding: "The refugee problem should not be considered as being confined to persons of any particular race or faith." See *While Six Million Died* by Arthur D. Morse.

21. "Approaching the Holocaust (*Judaism,* Winter 1973).

22. The source of this remark is in *Sefer Hayikarim.* Similar opinions were voiced by Saadia Gaon, Yehudah Halevi, and Reb Yedayah Hapnini. (That man's intellectual faculty cannot perceive God's essence.)

23. The argument, it seems to me, can be formulated as follows: What is logical, is not necessarily true; and what is true, is not necessarily logical.

VI

CONFESSION
(The Sense of Personal and Collective Guilt)

The heart of Holocaust poetry is permeated by a sense of guilt, especially in the poetry of non-victim authors although a similar feeling pervades the works of survivor writers too. The vicarious identification with the Holocaust martyrs and victims is psychologically shattering to the point of obsession. The authors imagine the sensation of gagging and gasping for air, or the tightening sensation of the noose. It is symptomatic of total empathy, remorse and compunction. These sorts of feelings are often transformed into mental pangs of guilt. They create a feeling of personal incompleteness and inferiority for not having been part of the actual suffering, anguish, agony and even death. This is the essence of the confession that is reflected in Holocaust poetry and besets the poet's mind and conscience. The wish to have had the "privilege" of sharing in the tragic lot of our people has been dramatically expressed:

> Ah, had I been let to walk together with you
> In your path of agony and torture
> And offer my neck in the noose-chain
> Like Jeremiah of old . . .
> Kissing the footsteps stained by blood
> Which sprinkled the ground
> Embrace your dripping wounds with kind hands
> And wipe your burning tears from off your faces.
> If I only had the privilege to stand with you
> When you were taken to be killed into the

Field of slaughter,
If only I could share with you
The fright of the abyss that faced you
Just before the bullet pierced you . . .

Daily I wish I could inmmerse with you
My life with yours in bitterness, curse,
Shame and aversion
And daily I would toxicate myself
With your dolor
And daily I would sanctify and purify
Myself in you.

— Ephraim Lisitzky, "Ho, Me Itneni Tzoed"

The key to the "confession" theme is defined in one verse: "Had I only been allowed to suffer in your stead." This soul-stirring wish has no equivocation whatsoever. It is cogently clear. There is no trace of rhetoric or abstractions. For this reason, we ought to credit the poets, each according to his or her poetic genre, for their sincere effort to project authentic empathy with their dying people in the grip of Nazi atrocities. In fact, they succeeded in expressing their feelings most convincingly and in internalizing them, as well as eternalizing this apocalyptic horror in the poetic verse.

Many poets present us with their particular sense of guilt-feeling, empathy and identification with the fate that befell their brethren. Oft times, their personal emotions break forth with rage as they chastise themselves, revealing the depth of their own anguish and vicarious reliving of the Holocaust nightmare. Often they descend, in their imagination, with their people into the valley of death:

With those that went to their death,
My own foot-steps joined them too.

With those that went to their death,
All my years went too,

With those that went to their death,
All my dreams went with them too.
I went with them,
With my brethren,
The humiliated.

Soiled with the excrement of the Satan.
The last of the human race,
The servants of the Lord
The messengers of the Messiah!

— Yitzchak Ogen, "Al Gesher Halal"

Between the poet who wishes to relive the marytrs' experiences, trodding with his brethren towards the gas chamber, and the one who yearns, although vicariously, to replace his brethren in their agony, there stands the third character who affirms his existential reality but detests it. He claims that he no longer can resume the pursuit of a normal existence in view of the Auschwitz horrors. He can no longer eat to satiety, nor sleep unperturbed, nor live fully day by day:

In this very moment
When I inhale
A lungful of air —
Upon the devastated plains of desolated Poland
Roll railroad cars filled with deadly gases.
And in the wagons there are riding
My brothers and sisters, old and young
Crowded in darkness
And with their bloody fingernails
They scratch on the impenetrable walls:
AIR, AIR!
And in the choking spasm
They exhale their life . . . breathe their last . . .
In that moment
As I feast my eyes on the celestial splendor
In this very moment
When I inhale
A lungful of air —
Upon the devastated plains of desolated Poland
Roll railroad cars filled with deadly gases.
And in the wagons there are riding
My brothers and sisters, old and young
Crowded in darkness
And with their bloody fingernails
They scratch on the impenetrable walls:
AIR, AIR!
And in the choking spasm
They exhale their life . . . breathe their last . . .

In that moment
As I feast my eyes on the celestial splendor
In the fields of desolated Poland
Deep and dark ditches are being dug
To throw into them like garbage on a dump
My brothers and sisters, old and young
Slaughtered, electrocuted and poisoned.
And there are times when the ground will tremble
From above the pits,
From the spasms of those who were buried alive.

In this very moment on my bed
When I rest from the day's toil —
In the Ghettos of desolated Poland,
The remnants of my brothers and sisters

Are scared of the slightest commotion —
"The Hangmen are coming . . ."?
And the mother hugs her babe to her breast
The grandmother her grandchild
The father a son, and brother his brother
Trembling they hold on to each other . . .
And weeping . . . And silence . . .
And fear is felt . . .
In this very moment . . .

— David Shimoni, *Shirim,* Vol. 2

This poem reflects an unusual attempt at empathy as well as a serious endeavor to integrate the poet's personal life with that of the Holocaust events of nightmare, torture, suffering, anxiety and despair. The *Shoah* nightmare holds sway over the entire framework of his life. In short, he tries to live it, feel it and even vicariously experience it. He does it by capturing a microscopic moment of the *Shoah* terror, and concentrates in its static tense the entire essence of the Holocaust apocalypse. In that particular moment, he is in a sort of Holocaust trance and experiences phenomenologically the *Dinge-An-Sich* as it were, or an unusual awareness of what has occurred in that horrifying happening, in the theatre of infernal death and Dantesque torture.

Wherever I go, I hear footsteps.

Wherever I stand I hear rattling
— My brothers in prison,
In the cells of depressing grief . . .

Every time I lie down I hear
— The sounds of my brethren
Herded to the slaughter . . .
From out the brands of conflagration
From out the debris of the ruins
From out the cities and hamlets — altars for sacrifices;
The groan of their extermination
Terrifies my nights
And my eyes never cease seeing them before me,
And my heart will not desist from shouting:
ABOMINATION!

— Shin Shalom, "Kechol She'elech"

This motif of personal identification, so dominant in the poet's confessions, has been skillfully summarized by Enda Amir in her poem "Shvuah" (The Oath):

When we lie down and when we rise up
Your terror we shall live,
The fire-burns that were seared into your flesh
Were also branded into ours.

Accordingly, the *Shoah* tragedy has left its profound scar upon every Jewish heart.

Another poet puts it this way:

You are the tense string
Unto which grief and silence cling
Your skin is flayed
You are sinews and a mouth
You are the soul of the wound

Only to you come the chained
The sighs and the voice

Your sons are murdered daily
Upon a stone

You are an open grave
Within you they are resurrected
In the form of this destitution.

— Aharon Apfelfeld, "Molad"

The Holocaust horrors captivate the poet and peradventure, the oppressiveness of his guilty conscience gnaws at him, and becomes in a way more anguishing than those with firsthand personal experiences of the Holocaust terrors.

How can I sit down to a meal
And how can I embrace a body,
How can I laugh and hear laughter,
How can I live the life of a beast

How can I sing from a full heart,
How can I even utter the word: beautiful?

— Uri Tzvi Greenberg, "Rechovot Hanahar"

The reaction of the poets to the Holocaust excesses was not only through their meditative confessionals and personal identification, but also in their refusal to reconcile themselves with the fact that they were far away from the Holocaust scene. The greater their geographical distance from the Holocaust scene, the greater was their pain of separation from their brethren to whom they were so spiritually close and committed:

For the sin I committed,
My brother in the crematorium
For I felt
The burning of your heart
From afar . . .

— Shin Shalom, "Al Cheyt"

Because of this awareness of the distance that separated the persecuted from the elegizers and the incomparable difference in experiences, the poet simulates in his own mind a living image of his people which remained imbedded in his subconscience. Thus:

Every time I speak of them —
My insides turn within me.
I cannot subdue
My sense of grief and calamity.
I remember them well
I set them before my eyes
They will never depart from me
In my joys and grief.
Every cry and lament
Is an everlasting echo
Of their last outcry.

— Reuben Weintraub, "Midey Dabri Bam"

These pathological consternations eventually turn into scorching flagellations of self-accusation. This may be, indeed, psychologically salutary. Ventilation of emotions is desirable. For had it been otherwise, the poets would have no other recourse but to run the streets of the world in sackcloth and ashes summoning a phlegmatic mankind to fasting.

One poet confesses:

Alas, forgive me my insulted brothers
I eat my daily bread to satisfaction
How come it has not yet stuck in my throat? . . .

How come that my soft mattress
Did not turn into a bed of thorns
To hurt and scratch my body? . . .

How come my heart is not chewed up
From the shame of those extirpated
From their human source?

Forgive me my brothers!

— Ephraim Lisitzky, "Ho Silchu Li"

There are the cases when the poet is guilt-ridden for having saved himself, even though he did not escape but went as an idealist to Zion:

Why have I abandoned you, my brothers

Alas, Why?
At a time when you were in distress
Facing the open abyss,
When the raging storm broke forth
When the stormy night was wailing,
And I did not remain
Between the dead and the living . . .
Why have I abandoned you
When God unleashed
His wrath upon His people?
Why have I not remained
With you in trouble
Until our suffering
Would have been declared: Enough!

— Pinchas Peli, "Lamah Azavtichem"

Since confession is usually introspective in nature, the poets often reach deep into their own souls and psyches. They soon discover that the Auschwitz nightmare disturbs them deeply and incessantly. They begin feeling like martyrs who subconsciously demand of themselves to appear in the role of "The Servant of the Lord" who is supposed to be carrying the entire burden of his people's suffering, being prepared to offer himself on God's altar for the sake of his people:

Heavens, carry a prayer-offering in song for me
If I was destined from birth to be a sacrifice,
If I was to be bound like a sheep,
The way I was already —
I am truly fortunate!
Let them do the murdering
And I will turn to my Lord;
Please don't lament for me —
Heavens, carry a prayer-song for me!

— Aharon Zeitlin, "Shir Ha'akedah"

Like Shin Shalom, who in one of his poems immolates himself in view of his people's annihilation (*M'chol Bashalshalaot*) so does the poetess Enda Amir see herself as a complete sacrifice not only *with* her people, but also *for* her people.

For your spilled blood into my heart flowed
Through a thousand channels,
Your torture was mine
And I was burned together with you,
With everyone tortured on the wheel
I was there too
Every baby that was crushed
Was as mine own flesh and blood, —
I am your complete sacrifice
My people Israel.
I was scorched and purified
From every foreign dross;
Indeed, I am nothing but a beacon
Yet your light shines for a distance,
Yet your call is heard from afar.

She takes upon herself the task to tell our tragedy in the name of the immolated and the tortured from the vantage point of self denial:

And ablaze I am
And nothing of me remains,
Nothing but a beacon unto you
My people Israel.

Self-denouncement, remorsefulness and readiness to be sacrificed for the nation are most honorable deeds. Nothing seems to supercede them. Yet there is till another step which transcends every form of empathy: a fervent wish to be lacerated together with one's people by the same hand of the Lord, after having regretfully discovered that "there is no sanctity in suffering" when realizing that the "groaning cry of the bleeding to death" is a futile last effort.

And while my brethren are being lacerated
With iron combs
And their anguished cries go unheeded,
And I sit here in the grace of the sun —
Punish me, Lord, with Your murderous hand,
Smite me with confusion
And feverish delirium
And crush me like a worm.
And while Jewish eyes are being pierced
And broken arms splinter in the streets

In the molars of a dog —
Listen, please, Lord to this Satanic prayer:
May my skull be broken
And my two eyes burst
And leak out their light drip by drip . . .

And while a wife in the arms of her husband
Is choked to death in the grave
And while I write poems to the glory of the blue skies:
Send me too to the slaughter
In the most honorable place in town
And let me too feel the touch of the knife.

— Avigdor Hameiri, "Heyd Mitofet"

The poets seem to feel a deep frustration for not having also been victims of the Holocaust. Empathy seems not to be enough. There was a profound desire to have shared the doleful fate of our people. There was, as already mentioned, a sense of incomplete Jewishness. They saw in every victim and survivor of the Holocaust experience a Rabbi Akiva, the personification of the complete Jew who rejoiced in his martyrdom, feeling completely fulfilled as a Jew who served God by offering his life on the nation's altar with "all his heart and soul." The great Yiddish poet H. Leivick immortalized his feelings on this very subject in his famous poem 'A Treblinka Candidate":

I was not in Treblinka
Nor in Maidanek.
But I stand at their entrance,
On the threshold of the gas chambers.
The threshold — God's wide world
The porch — The world-to-come:
Thusly, I stand and wait for your command
Great world:
A Jewish head for the gas chamber!
Everything around is so divinely splendid
Forests shake their pious heads
Over mountains and deserts,
Winds rise in a swirling dance.
The sun-so bright and fiery
Fed by the fires of Maidanek.

In my life-time
I was invited many times
To die at the pleasure of inquisition-tortures.
And I stand so in line
At the entrance
Of the World's Concentration Camp
A marked candidate for Treblinki.

Natan Alterman put is this way:

With the people that gave me
Tears and laughter
We too faced death together with them . . .

— Hatur Hashvi'i, Vol. 1

The nobility of the poet's wish and identification is impressive. It is only a wish, but no one has the right to minimize this sort of empathy. Nevertheless, there were those who frowned upon this sort of thing. This is a most sensitive subject and we shall discuss it later in this chapter.

In these several examples, we have seen how the poets revealed their deep personal sorrow and anguish with the Holocaust victims. The personal feelings of the authors are important since they help us perceive their poetry as an extension of their innermost feelings and the sense of their people's annihilation as a personal tragedy. *More than any other subject, the Holocaust topic requires emotional and spiritual involvement in order to attain a measure of authenticity. In short, identification with and deep understanding of the Holocaust are basic prerequisites for dealing with this awesome subject.*

Thus, it should not come as a surprise that the authors have great difficulties in handling the Holocaust topic in all the literary forms. Their perplexity stems from the pangs of conscience of many who were not in Auschwitz yet felt the burden of moral and national responsibility to accord the Holocaust subject the prominence it so tragically deserves.

Uppermost was the psychological question as to how much nerve one needs to possess in order to write and describe one's own tragedy. There was also the doubt as to whether a nonparticipant was worthy of delving into this sacred and awesome chapter of the *Shoah.*

And, finally, how could one grasp the enormity of the Holocaust horror?

M. Wolfson addressed this issue quite bluntly. He wrote: "Let us admit and confess, admit and be embarrassed . . . before our generation and the generation to come. We have not grasped the enormity of the extermination horror . . . the great and awesome destruction . . . We have not apprehended an all embracing perception . . . neither emotionally, intuitively or intellectually . . ." (*Moznayim* Iyar, 5707). Regardless of the argument, David Shimoni attempts to defend the compulsion of the poet to touch upon the Holocaust theme:

> And your son won't ask,
> Nor will he be surprised
> Why the poet failed to erect
> A monument to the Holocaust
> To this terror which has no precedence.
>
> For as long as a divine spark
> Still whispers within him,
> For as long as his heart is not petrified
> Your son already guessed
> He understood already
> That from this incomparable horror,
> Every voice and sound
> Were choking in the throat,
> Every cry, every eulogy turned mute.
>
> — "Ubincha Lo Yishal"

Shimoni voices here his honest doubt as to whether he is capable of offering a proper expression of the unprecedented tragedy. He comforts himself with the hope that his sons will not raise the issue of the poet's silence, since they will learn to understand how the subject rendered the poet "exhausted by tears and bereft of lament" . . . One can fully appreciate this internal struggle of the poet and his self-doubt. Yet the Holocaust subject became, unto itself, the supreme challenge, that awaits resolution . . .

Shin Shalom, however, refuses to retreat from this awesome challenge. He is ready to confront it, yet he poses the question with fatherly concern:

My son, do you know . . .
Do you hear . . .
Do you understand . . .
Do you sense . . .
What is happening today . . .
What sort of verdict is being meted out today?

— *Shirim*

As a consequence of self-doubt and merit to deal with the Holocaust topic, the logical question arises whether it may not be best to be silent, altogether:

I will then enter the covenant of silence
Into the secret of the seraphim of terror,
I will prostrate myself to the storm of my heart
Which is chained to the moorings of silence . . .
That which was sealed
With the mouth in fire
I will enter a cliff and hide,
Until wickedness will end in the world.

— Abraham Broides, "Shorashim Basela"

"At such a time the prudent keeps silent" (*Amos* V:13) whispers, as it were, the wind of the times, in the ears of the poet, and thus he reacts within his spiritual confusion:

It is better to be silent
In these pandemonic days
And like a sailor on high seas
Hope to discover some enchanted shores.

— Shaul Raz, "Tiferet Yichudeynu"

The idea of silence did not please the poets. They knew well that silence is not always a sacred act, although they did not delude themselves as to the enormity of the Holocaust subject, its scope and its implied responsibility.

Aharon Zeitlin in the introduction to his poem "On the Ashes of A Consumed Nation" declared that were Jeremiah alive during the Holocaust era "in this darkness of annihilation", he surely would have been overcome by the inhuman atrocities to enable him to lament over the ashes of his destroyed nation:

Would that God Himself had tried
To rob from His mouth
The cry for help — and He could not.
Like the eternal silence of forgotten millions
So would the son-of-Hilkiyah have remained silent
In the presence of the Lord.
Now even the outcry is worthless
All tears turned into script
All prayers are in vain . . .

— Aharon Zeitlin

Even if God had forced him to elegize, Jeremiah would have remained steadfast in his silence in the face of the indescribable horror. He would have been bereft of proper expressions to describe this terrifying devastation of life. It obtains, therefore, that silence can be interpreted as rebellion against the God who forces one to speak. At any rate, at the beginning of the Nazi atrocities, even though the reaction was immediate, the general stunning silence was much too obvious:

It seems to me
That everybody has pledged
To silence the tears forever.

— Tzvi Arad, "Yoman Ba'efer"

But the silence could not continue *ad infinitum.* It was condemned:

And the heart trembles within
In these days of gloom:
How did this silence come about
And why?
Where is the shriek against the terror
Where is our outcry
The cry for help of the dying
For all the times?

— B. Mordecai, "Shirat Ha'eden He'avud"

But this poetic silence was symptomatic as noted already. Great hesitation pervaded its authors. There was fear of failing to express adequately and doubt in one's ability to measure up to the task let alone the futility of the effort:

And with your eyes
Our eyes see,
And with your ear
Our ear hears:
The horror cry
The slaughter
The burning
And the trembling . . .

— Shin Shalom, *Shirim*

Here then we have true testimony by the poet and his colleagues through whose concerted effort the people were made to perceive the frightening scope of the *Shoah* and to tell what it really meant:

Upon one's lips
Comes up the number:
Six million!

— Ibid

The poet Abraham Shlonsky also apologized for his inability to treat adequately the great tragedy of our people:

I cannot endure it any longer
Nor can I cry!
Shut the light or dim the eyes!
The darkness sets in! —
And I shall wail sevenfold
And I don't know which is what:
NEBO or EBAL?

And I don't know: EBAL or NEBO?
That's silence —
To cry —
I don't know how to name it.
That's how a storm can be silent:

For it never occurred
That's how a storm can alarm:
Which is about to arrive!

— *Shirim,* Vol. II

The aforementioned trepidation in confronting the Holocaust has many variations:

My pen I dip in blood
My litany I'll kindle in the pyre
In a sea of blood and accursed fire.
There isn't a fitting sound,
Nor a word or a phrase
To express a man's pains from torture
And of a people
Trampling and choking in its own blood.

My pen I dip in blood,
How can I convert my pain into words?
My poem has been silenced by the thunders
Around me.
Orphaned, lonesome and confused
I hide from making a sound
I convulsively jump like a wounded bird
That bites its lip instead of moaning
The poem served me as a litany,
The dirge turned into supplication,
The outpouring of a man's heart within himself,
For his God is neither merciful nor gracious.

Why have You, Lord, made it bitter for me,
Destroying every sound of joy
On the strings of my heart
Granting me ululations, that's all?
I dip my pen in blood,
And sacred is this spilled blood,
I am ashamed to dip my pen in it
And polish with it eloquent expressions.
Spilled blood has no rhyme
Nor is there a word that is authorized to atone
For a shed tear, sigh and cry.
Blood has its own language:

Each sound is saturated with
Bereavement and orphanhood.
It cries out from the ground
And the sound of its moan
Will never cease.

— Mordecai Tenenboim, "B'cheret Dvay"

In Teneboim's footsteps come others to express similar difficulties:

Woe! There are no more words in my mouth
In view of the upheavals
Tens of thousands are being destroyed
And no end to the suffering is in sight.

— Menachem Bergman, "Ben Ha'aretz"

Meir Mohar offers an explanation of the difficulties encountered by the authors:

The anguish refuses to be cast into language . . .
It always evades its yoke
And prefers to play to its utter capacity . . .
The mute will buffet its victim
Despairing of the mercy of expression
Hollow in the echo of his sob
In which his grief does partake . . .

— *Hadoar,* Vol. 19, 5700

In spite of the prevalent emotional dilemma faced by the authors as to whether or not they were morally entitled to deal with the Holocaust subject, they were impelled to write by the profound awareness that this unfortunate generation of survivors has the sacred obligation to put down on paper, in whatever form, everything pertaining to the *Shoah* so that future generations may know and not forget.

Poetry had a special reason to address the Holocaust theme. There was a well founded awareness, a sort of truism, that man may be gone but his poem will survive and serve as a living witness and testify to the events.

Thus, the anonymous Ghetto poet:

And if life was lost
The dirge of grief will not be wasted
It will live in the generations to come.

— *Prager Anthology*

With still greater impetus, Yitzchak Katzenelson adopted poetry's Commandment to perpetuate in verse the horror story of our people's annihilation. In the introduction to his epic: "The Song of the Slaughtered Jewish People" he jotted down his own last testament in words saturated with the blood of his anguished heart:

Sing please!
Take your harp in your hand . . .

Pluck with your heavy fingers
Every string . . .
Every finger is like a grieving heart . . .
Carry your last song
About the last Jews
On European earth . . .

Sing once more the last song on earth . . .
And for the last time sing him a song,
Awaken your harp with the sound of triumph:
All Jews are annihilated, they are no more
They were killed, massacred, and gone!

Much has been written about the *Shoah* and in connection with the *Shoah*. In fact, the Holocaust subject has been treated by writers and poets whose majority has been at best "dilettantish," and by a distinct minority of known authors and poets. However, What seemed to be of paramount importance was the conscious awareness of the writers of their historic responsibility to record, to tell, to write. Poetry did its share in its particular responsibility to perpetuate the story of our anguish in verse. The latter was the essential thought that governed this gallant effort, but for some of the elitist purists it was just too much to tolerate:

Like a tempest we were flooded

With poems of woe,
The anguish of pain
Mumbled in words
And pain without form —
Woe unto me!

Poets, dilettantes and verse makers
Each with his own pick
Like digging for gold
To put in their bag
From the storage of grief
And to leave their name
In a book or a brief.

In every inn and language
Every stammerer and lame one
Comes with his hoarse Kaddish
On the graves
To pervert every word
And to desecrate the tear
When the vulture descends
Upon the cadavers . . .

— M. Domnitz, "V'acharey He'ason"

And Shimon Ben-Eliezer takes the dilettantes to task with a tirade:

You had enough you shedders of tears
Your lyric grates on my ears
Who can tolerate the sound
Of your lament over my misfortune?

What of your profuse wail and moan
Adding more eulogies upon our sorrow?
Are you so desirous of wounds and destruction
Or do you enjoy suffering?

Don't give me details about the disaster,
I, too, was orphaned.
The aspirations of my youth were buried,
Together with you I received no mercy.
Don't prattle like an ignoramus
Who brags with empty slogans,

For he who suffered as we did
Will loathe eloquent rhetoric.

Sorrow may tranquilize
Wailing will stupefy.
When the time of confusion arrives,
It will pleasingly comfort the fool.

Every idler without ability
Bitterly laments you his chest.
How facile it is to wail in comfort
While ensconced with folded arms.

— "K'neged Hamekonenim"

This sort of scathing and indisciminate sweeping criticism of the Holocaust writers in general and of poetry in particular seems insensitive, myopic and unjustified. It betrays a lack of historic perspective. It fails to take into account the many important contributions of these literary and pseudo-literary materials toward a more perceptive understanding of the Holocaust nightmare.

In 1948, a painful dispute ensued in the Israeli press[2] led by Dr. Israel Rubin. regarding, what he termed the "Graphomania" literature of the Holocaust and post-Holocaust period. He dismissed the writers who, themselves victims of the Holocaust, lacked any appreciable literary skill, thus failing to offer an "artisitc" expression of the *Shoah.* He accused them of offering nothing but stories of the Shoah tragedy as they experienced it with all its attendant horrible details. He admitted, as an evident afterthought, that those who have ventured to jot down the facts of their agony for the benefit of future generations may really know what has occurred in the Nazi hell, but cannot be expected to provide literary art.

However, he continued his tirade, once they survived and sat down to write chronicles of the events as they remembered them, in autobiographies and the like, they produced nothing but "graphomania," which, in his view, gave only personal satisfaction to the authors, but contributed little to the story of the Holocaust, for all these writings were emotional outlets for the bloody wounds of their past.

Ephraim Shmueli,[3] did not fail to inveigh, with moral justification, against this callous criticism of Rubin. He admitted that there was no literary art to be found in the various forms of the Holocaust literature. He rightly asked whether there was any evidence of literary art in the chronicles of the medieval period and in its poetry and stories. Was Notte Hanover a skilled historian? Of what artistic value was the poetry of Rabbi Hakim, Shlomo Ben Shimshon and others? Yet their literary legacy has remained of invaluable historic import. Nachum Sokolov, in his day, observed that neither Yehudah Leib Gordon's epic poem "Beyn Shiney Arayot" or Chaim Nachman Bialik's "B'ir Ha'Hareygah" were great literary achievements. Yet regardless of their artistic value, they will remain the great historic epic stories of our people. The historic value of the writings establish and secure their lasting fame.

Hence, what more can be said when the real poets and chroniclers of the Holocaust were the very victims or distant, but spiritually close, witnesses to the tragedy of the *Shoah?*

Michael Wyschograd is correct in his observation that "any attempt to transform the Holocaust (tragedy) into (literary) art demeans (in fact) the Holocaust . . . If at all, art is a rebellion against everything temporary, fleeting and ephemeral, perhaps we ought to see in the written legacy of the Holocaust a new form of art which preserves "the source of its emotions."[4] In a similar sense, Lawrence Langer was on target in his study *The Holocaust and the Literary Imagination* by stressing that since literature "aspires toward the revelation of a new sense of reality" Holocaust literature does not have to aspire, for it contains a new reality capable of convincingly presenting it to the reading public.

The victim writer is intrinsically a bearer of living testimony in one form or another. He does not need to convince. Yet says Josephine Knopp "The Holocaust writer — virtually alone among writers — faces the difficulty of making a factual subject believable, of informing the actuality he describes with an aura of reality acceptable to his readers. Therefore, the true mission of Holocaust literature lies not in Aristotelian catharsis . . . but rather in urgent need to break through the barrier of non-acceptance engendered by an absence of that core of shared experience and sensibility upon which other literature may rely . . . For this reason, continues Dr. Knopp, "only those who have experienced it (The Holocaust) first hand can produce literature which transmits the Holocaust Universe authentically."[5]

Bearing in mind the aforesaid, one may well have a much greater appreciation of the inner struggle of the poets who felt spiritually and emotionally compelled to venture into the Holocaust subject. Thus writes Uri Tzvi Greenberg:

> The divine presence of the Hebrew Poem
> Stands over its victims on Sinai
> Beholds the sea and the continent of the nations
> Now — it recites the holy dirge
> Over its slaughtered and living people.
>
> — "Rehovot Hanahar"

While the world may indeed be waiting for the great threnodists, as U.Z. Greenberg maintains, the Hebrew poet lives in the grip of:

> I have set Maidanek
> Before me forever,
> I have set Messiah
> Before me forever . . .
>
> — Aharon Zeitlin, "Beyn Ha'esh Vehayesha"

Hence, the words of M. Margalit become clearer when he says:

> It is impossible otherwise,
> Woe unto the Jewish people,
> For the crown fell from its glorious head.
> Even when they pass
> The restored city,
> Their spilled blood — has no rest yet,
> (All is left) but to jot down:
> JERUSALEM, ZION
> AND SIX MILLION! . . .
>
> — *Beyt Ya'akov,* Vol. 24, 5721

In this further poetic soul-searching struggle and personal confrontation with the awesome subject of the Holocaust, the poet, as if assuring himself, pleads with his muse:

> My poem, don't be embarrassed
> And my voice, refrain from being silent!
>
> — Avraham Broides, "Sharashim Basela"

Or the confession of the poetess who admits:

All the words come —
They yearn to offer a threnody
Dried up they return, and lonely
Even the cry retreats
In silent madness . . .

Rahel Negev, "Yizkor"

Yet there continues the incesant urge to peg down these yet unredeemed words, to bear testimony and immortalize the truth:

To cry out once more
Before falling prey to the passage of time,
To smash the fences with the forehead,
With my fingernails I'll inscribe on the wall
This testament of mine unto eternity.

— Zvi Arad, "Yoman Ba'efer"

In short, this question of conscience to write down everything that needs to be said in spite of one's personal trepidation has been overcome by the awareness of the authors of their historic obligation towards their people, to perpetuate the memory of the *Shoah.* For this reason, our poetry has been immensely enriched in all aspects. Above all, its content was the overriding factor, not its artisitic expression nor its poetic form.

Up until now we addressed the matter of the prevalent self-doubt of the poets in their personal confrontation with the appalling subject of the Holocaust. This constituted the essence of their own self-confessions.

Before we conclude this chapter we should take note of the subject of collective confessions which have occupied a prominent place within the subject on hand. Those authors in particular who were spared the Nazi rod were remarkably outspoken and direct in a manner we have not encountered when the confession was of personal character. The collective confession has been summarized in Abraham Holtz's "Confession in the Memory of the Six Million":

For the sin which we committed before you

And before them:
By refusing to hear . . .
By not using our power . . .
By being overcautious . . .
By hesitating . . .
By useless conferences . . .
By senselessness . . .
By betraying brothers . . .
By being complacent in those times . . .

Frankly, this chapter is too painful to delve into these murky details. The record speaks for itself, a record of collective awareness, lack of confidence, insensitivity and indetermination. Jewry outside the reach of the Nazi claws failed itself and failed us in the throes of death.

Israel Efros, the Hebrew poet who resided in America, remembers well the early beginnings of the Nazi onslaught, and speaks with agonizing pain and utter disgust with the then leadership of American Jewry:

I came with thousands of Jews
(To Madison Square Garden)
To hear the cry of our hearts
And in its echo to detect
A sign of strength
Of a healthy collective in anguish
That can mitigate its own pain;
But my pitiful sorrow
Spread itself upon the walls . . .

One by one the leaders rose
And each word of theirs felt
Like burning coal in my ears:
Our heart full of love to the nation
Endowed with the great spirit
Cultivated on capriciousness,
On Goethe and Schiller.
There was no hate in our mouth,
No demand for revenge . . .
Where have you learned
These alien ideas?
Who made you saints

At the expense of other lives?
Who diminished your power to roar . . .
Who muffled your outcry
To match our calamity
Which may refract on the heavenly drum
And fall like heavy hammers
On the hearts of all living things?
Who weakened your fists
And dissovled your anger
And silenced the glorious thunders
Of your souls?
Do you remember?
"Fortunate is he
Who can attack and smash . . ."

— "Anachunu Hador"

The future historian will have to assess the collective behavior of American Jewry in those tragic days. Nor will the leadership of the Yishuv in Palestine and the Yishuv itself be spared the judgment of the future historian.

The Hebrew poet of the Yishuv, Ya'akov Fichman, did not fail to mark this truth:

How could thousands delude themselves
At the mouth of the crater,
How come the storm failed
To alarm the people to revolt,
To love, to liberate the oppressed! . . .

— *K'tavim*

Fichman returns to the same subject in another of his poems hinting that within their own enclave "between the walls" neither brother nor friend are alert to see what is happening around them. "The scouts are tardy", the watchmen are not on their posts . . ."

The abyssmal failure of the "free world" Jews to rush to rescue their brothers, did not ahsolve the victimized European Jewish Community for its lack of foresight, or intuition of the forboding signs before the outbreak of the Nazi onslaught. Meir Bossak, himself a victim and survivor, is burdened with oppressive self-guilt and self-accusation for his own failure not to have seen the coming of our destruction, nor does he spare his critical rod from his own martyred brothers. He bemoans the fact that there was ample time to save great numbers from annihilation. He claims that Euorpean Jewry could have gone on mass Aliyah but no one moved until Hilter came and liquidated us through the gas chambers. He reflects that the "Messiah" walked the streets of Europe "with a torch" warning the people of the oncoming tragedy, but nobody paid any attention:

That hour we knew
That the bridge to tomorrow
Was broken.

— "Mul Kochavim"

Ya'akov Cahan thus reflected and asked:

And perhaps it is our own fault
We have prolonged only our life
But have done nothing to hasten "the End",
To force open the gates of redemption
For which we hoped and longed
And for God's kingship,
And we kept silent in the face of wickedness
And almost made peace with our enslavement
And weak and weary we allowed evil
To rise and spread until it ran all over us . . .
Indeed, You have castigated us O Lord
More than enough! . . .

— *K'tavim*

And in another place Cahan writes:

We too have been guilty, rebellious,
And have sinned much too much!
For having neglected our Covenant
And we took our children
And sacrificed them to alien nations —

We have sinned much too much!
To say: There is light among the nations,
The light of charity,

And we shall live in their shadow —
We have transgressed, indeed! . . .

— Ibid

We have seen that no one was spared chastisement and castigation. Neither the individual nor the collective. Each received his deserved criticism.

In short, the tremors of the Holocaust are continuously felt and they will continue for as long as the conscience of man will be burdened with the question: How could a tragedy such as the Holocaust have been planned, and executed in full view of the Western World?

NOTES

1. Compare Fichman: *Pe'at Sadeh*

   We are the only remnants
   Of the world's Holocaust
   And unto the very end
   We shall bewail this conflagration.

   OR

   In this great fire
   We were consumed too.
2. *Al Hamishmar,* October 12, 1948.
3. *Ibid.* December 24, 1948.
4. Michael Wyschograd, *Sh'ma,* April 29, 1977.
5. Ibid.

VII

UNSHAKEN FAITH

In Chapter V, "Complaint Against Heaven." we have seen that in spite of the seemingly belligerent tone, the assault against Heaven was rooted in the classical spirit of Judaism's dialogue with God and in the ground of Israel's faith. We have also indicated that most of the Jewish masses went to their deaths in silent protest without either renouncing or denouncing their faith in Israel or God.

In this chapter we shall demonstrate this fact through the poetic selections which testify to this extrordinary Jewish loyalty, unshakeable faith, and religious feeling in its various manifestations in the face of the horrendous Nazi cataclysm.

This unique faith of ours has been summarized in the following short poem:

Without faith in
The Almighty God
What value and meaning
Have all my deeds?

Without trust
In imminent redemption
There is no good reason to live
One additional moment.

— "B'eyn Emunah," *Prager Anthology*

As evidence of the prevailing spiritual attitude of the Jewish masses during this oppressive period, two of the most popular songs were:

a) Maimonides' Thirteenth Principle of Faith:

"I believe in the coming of the Messiah, and if he tarries, nevertheless, I shall wait every day until he arrives."

— *Ani Ma'amin*

b) The statement, Isaiah VIII:10

"Hatch a plot — It shall be foiled;
Agree on action — It shall not succeed.
For with us is the Lord."

— Utzu Eytza

Thus, in the midst of great suffering and still greater fear of a threatening future and impending death, and in spite of the outcries of protest and skepticism if not, in some cases, actually blasphemous denunciations and vitriolic sarcasm, the deep running source of profound faith has been dominant within the masses, and, as reflected in the poetry of the Shoah, its corroborating witness.[1] It is a fact that the doomed masses in face of impending extermination, nevertheless entertained a sincere hope that they would be rescued in some manner from total annihilation. If rescue did not materialize, then hope surely helped preserve a sense of sanity and even courage to die with Jewish dignity and in definance of our enemies whose aim was not only to destroy physically the Jewish population, but also to eradicate the Jewish factor: namely, the Jewish spirit.

The Nazis had done everything in their power to reduce the Jewish masses to a state of total mental and spiritual derangement in order to justify the eradication of a "subhuman species" which deserved no ethical compunction nor moral doubt. In the midst of conditions so conducive to nihilism, agnosticism and denial there arose, in fact, a movement that preached repentance and piety as fantastic or paradoxical as it may sound to the outside observer. Out of this great despair the voice of courage and faith was heard most clearly:

Do not despair, brothers in distress
Even though God's rescue is mysterious
It may appear before us tomorrow!
With joy and zealous pride
Carry on the heavy burden

For this is the last of our misery.

Gladly we shall march on,
With the pride of an eternal people
In rain and in cold
Listen carefully to the forest-trees
They murmur: just a while longer
And the voice of good tidings will resound!

— "Al Ye'ush," *Prager Anthology*

Still more poignantly one hears the type of faith the people lived by in the simple verse of this entreaty written in the accents of the Holocaust nightmare:

Lord, our Father, have mercy
Hasten the end, we beseech You.
Bring about the end of our infinite suffering
And redeem us from our exile at last!

Master of the Universe
Behold our wandering
In the cold and in rain
Naked and barefooted
Without shelter or help
Beaten and tortured
Without a ray of hope.
We shall no more
Your commandment ignore
Your true word
We will wholeheartedly obey
Let the Messiah finally come
And people and city will recognize and know
That You are the true Lord.

— "Avinu Rachem," *Prager Anthology*

The extraordinary role played by the Jewish woman in the tragic years will forever be remembered. She was the heroine of the Ghetto and a source of infinite courage in the torture camps. Her sacrifice readiness, her compassion, her endurance, her morality, and her piety are legendary. She was the rock of hope and comfort. In the

Ghetto she kept her household together and preserved the glow of the tradition even in days of relentless gloom, unsanitary conditions and depressing Ghetto squalor. It is to her eternal credit that she preserved and promoted our sanity and will to survive.

As an example, this following poem written in the Lodz Ghetto reflects the pious purity of the persecuted women of Israel:

Blessed be He and blessed be His name!
Wherever I come and go
Whenever I can, I do
Bless the Sabbath candles.

Even though there is no electricity in camp
And a match is not to be found
And it is forbidden to light a fire
Death by hanging for one who does . . .
I bless the Sabbath candles in the sunset
As you commanded, Lord, to fulfill Your behest.

Blessed be He and blessed be His name!
Return us,
Our Lord,
To our homes.
Redeem us
From our torture,
And may we merit to hear
The Kiddush-blessing recited by our husbands.

Master of the Universe,
May our broken hearts reach You.
Open in Your mercy the gates of Heaven
And send peace
To all Your creatures.

— Hinda Levi-Linser, *Ani Ma'amin*

Mark Dvozetzky has written: "The religious poetry reflects the tragic state of mind which pervaded the Ghetto inmates, who were trapped in an unbearable condition with no possibility of escape."[2]

The following is a poem which mirrors in full measure the spirit of the faithful Jew. It reflects also that sort of piety which has not been oblivious to the reality and scope of our suffering. It testifies to the eternal covenant between Israel and its God and reflects the kind of faith which has preserved Israel from spiritual death through the contortions of a faith steeled in the crucible of Israel's fateful struggle to live and to believe . . .:

Hear, O Israel, the voice of my oath
Ascends to you from my seething blood
A cannibal people is slaughtering my children
And cooking their flesh before the eyes of the dying
If I am murdered, yet the one and only God lives
And in His name, my name and the name of my
Children will not die.
Hear, Israel — you are my heir,
And on Mt. Zion do not forget Mt. Sinai.
Earth and Heavens trembled at their vows,
Beholding our people expire on the gallows.
Hear Israel, will you ever forget them
Will you ever forget that you are their heir?
Will you forget, and if you betray—
Won't you be afraid on reckoning day?

Return Israel to your home, your faith
There is no other way . . .
Return to your Master . . .
No one else will be of help to you
Without Him, you are neither
A people nor a nation.
You are as naught . . .
Pardon I pray You the sin of the oppressed.
Remember when judging a rebellious father
Consumed by fire
The merit of his children.
And all the survivors of the furnace
Forgive please — that would be a just verdict
For You Who sits in Your heavenly hiding place.
Pardon us — alone in the forest
Still frightened from our experiences.
Remember unto us the soul that is still registered
In our name . . .
That pure soul stamped with the seal of this house
And if we survive at the edge of the bloody abyss,
In the torrent of wailing tears
Reimplant for us the seeds of light —

To have the sun shine again
In the valley of darkness
For otherwise what for have we survived?

And how can we kindle Thy light
In the heart of our children
If within us the light has been dimmed?
Therefore, pardon please, for the sake of their
Sacrifice
And in bestowing Your light upon us be with them.
Renew our spirit for the sake of their merit
And teach us Your truth,
For the sake of their truth . . .
Hear us, souls in Paradise,
The people of Torah will never cease,
For your bodies were slaughtered
And cremated in the land of murder,
But they have not died.
Scorched parchments — be comforted
The script is eternal, the truth remains forever.
Fragments of the Tablets — Rejoice
Torah is well and alive.

— Michel Dov Weissmandl, "Shma Israel"

Characteristic of those horrifying days by far not bereft of profound faith are the following verses where the interplay of liturgical language and traditional symbols convey the faith of the martyrs like a symphonic duet:

In the eventide of slaughter
Upheaval and extermination
I'll light the Havdalah candle
Of Israel's perennial separation.
Israel's fate — loneliness,
Its sanctity — supreme.
On the graves of its martyrs
God's light eternally shines.
The Gentile word — is dark
Its ways — deceit.
The rivers of separation
Are filled with blood.
The crucible of the ancient past

Served as the fiery testing ground
The Testament of the rebels is faith
I'm not afraid, I've no fear!

— Shaul Raz, "Havdalah"

According to the already mentioned Dvozetzky study a remarkably large amount of devotional and petitional poetry based on traditional liturgy appeared in every Ghetto center. These creations were the most popular: This is one example of many:

O Lord look at us from above and see
How we have become the derision of the foe
He looks at us like sheep for the slaughter
O Lord, how can You tolerate it?
We do not have any other friend
But You, the only one
And Your name is: The Guardian of Israel.

Therefore, to You we pray
Do not forget us Shomer Yisrael
Do not forget our tears, please . . .
For no one pays any attention to us
When we declare our faith in You!

Do not forget us, Guardian of Your flock
Show the nations that You are our God
We do not have anyone but You!
We have no other friend
But the one and only You!

— "Habet Mishamayim Ur'eh"

Not all poems of faith were of a plaintive nature. Some were by far not submissive. They turned, rather, into petitions for hopeful revenge:

Yitgadal Vyitkadash . . .
Glorified and Sanctified . . .
The tear has not dried yet
From mothers' faces
While the roads are strewn with death

And the blood has not yet congealed.
The corpses of our brothers
Still litter every hill and valley
Being trampled by haughty feet
Of human beasts — the enemy.

Here a hand wallows in blood
And there a skull is floating —
Silently, as it were, weeping for the
Horrifying destruction.
Only yesterday have I beheld peaceful homes
Today they became demolished dumps.
And the blue skies are beclouded by the
Billowing smoke.

Our home has been burned. The holy parchments
Are torn up by the despot
And the wicked hand of the defiled
Throws them into the fires.
The seared letters, indeed, are alighting,
Woe, when will the avenger come
To avenge their honor and the
Cry from the secret of generations?

The scum of humanity went on a rampage,
Wicked hands went wild,
Every hoodlum showers invectives on my sister
And every hooligan throws shoes at the elderly
Of my people
And heaps insults upon the memory of my prophets.

Grind your teeth, my brother,
Turn your groan into a stone,
Stop the blood rushing in your raging heart;
For retribution is reserved in the future
For those who perpetrated evil.
Don't be discourged, my brother:
The day of revenge will surely come!

— Noach P'niel, "Kaddish"

As with all other topics, here too one will clearly detect the difference in temper and background reference between the author who experienced the tragedy and the one who empathized with the tragedy although both have dealt with the same subject. Noach P'niel wrote in the Ghetto of Vilna with plaintive restraint while Michael Deshe wrote of bloody revenge in Caesaria in the Fall of 1943:

Sustain me, Lord, to reach
That chosen day
When I will wash my clean hands . . .
In the defiled blood
Of the progenitors of Sodom
Who murdered mothers with a smile
And slaughtered babies
With the calmness of Satan.

Strengthen me and support me my Lord,
For at the moment of sacred revenge
May my innocent hands not tremble . . .
When the groaning of my victims
Will resound in my ears . . .
The horror of my brothers
In the gas vans I will envision,
And those who dug their own graves
Will I recall . . .
And my anger will burn like a fire
And my only desire will be
To strike and crush my enemy . . .

The heavens above will have no peace
Nor the earth below any tranquility
Not until the last of the murderers
Will have atoned his crime
In his own contaminated blood
For the annihilation
Of my children and brothers . . .

Keep me alive, O Lord, for the day
Of rejoicing and glory
When my dimmed eyes will light up
And my being exult in the
Unfolding redemption story.

Awake my brothers in the hellish pit
Have hope, ye refugees from hell.

The day of freedom and retribution is near.
Rejoice, holy corpses
Let your bones chant in the grave
When your murderers will be destroyed . . .

Preserve me, O Lord, for that day!

— "T'filah L'el N'kamot"

Yes, amidst doubt, disappointment and rebelliousness there was steadfast faith. It expressed itself in various degrees and in strange ways. It often took on the character of unprecedented piety and zeal as a form of resisting the cruelest attempts to dehumanize the Ghetto or camp inmate as well as an act of defiance in face of inevitable death. It denied the Nazi-educated butchers the victory over the spirit of Israel. Thus faith in the Divine Promise was never lost. Actually, the way tradition was maintained and prayer services and Torah study continued uninterrupted were manifestations of a spiritual resurrection. These "dry bones" never lost their spiritual vigor. Furthermore, in the macabre drama of mass murder the people died with silent dignity bespeaking a martyrdom which could only be achieved because of profound faith.

For similar reasons, prayer was most prevelant in the Ghetto and the Death Camps. The mother prayed for bread for her starving baby and the orphan prayed for his murdered parents. One prayed for survival, another for merciful death.

One prayed for relief not to hear the anguished helpless groan nor to see the pain and torture that surrounded her on all sides. After all, how much is one expected to bear?

Hear my entreaty Lord
I am a Ghetto Jew —
Persecuted, lonely and poor.
My heart is shattered
Empty and gloomy
And I have no more prayers in me,
Hearken then to this last request . . .
Take away from me my human trait
Free me from Thy divine endowment
That I may not be touched
By the cry and sigh around me

Take my two ears, my Lord . . .
That I may no longer hear
The cry coming through the walls
Of every Ghetto house!
And take away the sight
From my eyes
That I may no longer behold
The cruel scenes
Of my brethren being
Led day and night
To their slaughter . . .
Turn me into a dog
That I may bite and
Tear apart Thy enemies
Dismembering them to the last bone! . . .
O Great God
Do with me as You please . . .
But do not form me again into a human being
Please . . .!

— "Eyn T'filot Li Yoter," *Prager Anthology*

This kind of prayer does not by far resemble the sort of supplications we have been used to. This was a typical prayer in the Ghetto, although incomprehensible to the normal mind outside the Holocaust.

Or take the prayer of the Ghetto thief. (How abnormal would it sound in this context to introduce any ethical postulates regarding the sin of stealing?) He prayed in sincere faith. He trusted God that his prayers would be answered. But the quintessence of his prayer reflected the great human tragedy and the intolerable conditions the Jews were manipulated into. A poor, wretched, orphaned, hungry youth on the run for life, he had to steal in order to survive. Many of us survivors still see this Ghetto picture in vivid dimensions — the nameless, homeless, abandoned, dehumanized Jewish boy in tatters. Who was he? Who were his parents? Nobody knew. He suddenly appeared among us fighting for life like the rest of us. He turned thief . . . and he faithfully prayed to God to help him survive . . . by stealing in order live . . .:

My body shrivels
From emaciation

Hunger is my father.
I am the Ghetto thief
A thief with a yellow badge.
In the morning dusk
When a wagon with fresh bread is passing
The heart is so famished
And the eyes from weeping tear.

Listen to me, O Lord, from on High,
I have never been a thief before,
But see how they gorge themselves
Like the gluttons with food
While others starve of hunger
And curse their bitter fate.

Hear me, O Lord,
Thy name is so sacred to me,
Grant me strength and dexterity
Eyes like fire
And feet faster than deer,
To enable me some food to acquire.

The police catch me with a bread in my hand
They beat me with sticks and a whip too,
I don't care whether I live or die
You see, what else can they do to me?

I jump the bread wagon and grab a bread,
They shout and yell
While my teeth are digging in . . .

Therefore, I thank You, Lord,
For the darkness of the nights
Which You have given me.
When everybody is sleeping
For me just begins
The struggle for life.

Thus forgive me, O Lord,
For my transgressions,
The world has chased me away from You.
A thief I became in the Ghetto

A hoodlum
Among men and human beasts . . .

— "T'filato Shel Ganav-Hagetto," *Prager Anthology*

In the following two examples the authors each offer a plea in the true sense of a dialogue with God. One pleads for God to rescue the remaining remnant while there is still time. Parenthetically speaking, what sense would God's redeeming power make if there was not one of the victims left? Indeed, what meaning would the Holocaust have taken on had Hitler and his Nazi gang succeeded to annihilate the very last Jew of Europe? Imagine if there were no surviving eyewitnesses. How would one suppose the Holocaust documents to have been read? Who would have had the audacity to interpret the tragedy? This is exactly the unpronounced gnawing issue in the field of Holocaust studies. The surviving victims must serve as living testimony. Those fortunate enough to have been spared the Holocaust agony have the obligation to assist in uncovering and recording the facts. Any interpretation of the Holocaust by those whose Holocaust experience goes not further than perhaps a visit to the ruins of the Auschwitz crematoria is fraught with misinterpretation.

The Holocaust is a terrifying phenomenal event of the Twentieth Century's monstrous achievement. The Holocaust is too horrendous and too mysterious, for want of a better term to be as yet interpreted; its ontological meaning is incomprehensible . . .

Suffering has reached
The intolerable level,
The victims are decaying . . .
And there is no end in sight
For a suffering people
Who waits for redemption . . .

Come, then, Our Redeemer,
Invoke Your saving power
If in Your design there is redemption
Do it now, at once
While You still have left
Some to rescue . . .
Here, no one hears our bitter prayer

It evaporates without reaching the sky
Are the gates of prayer locked indeed
For the pleas of the victims?

— *Ukvar Kashal Koach Hasevel*

On the other hand, the lyric poet Hillel Bavli struggles with the *mysterium tremendum.* He wants to touch the hem of the ultimate truth. His genuine religiosity encounters an insurmountable problem: how to still have faith in view of the Holocaust.

My Lord, broaden my perception
I entreat Thee
To carry the burden
Of my people's suffering;
To dive into the frightening abyss
With a fragile body,
To crawl in dust and still
Reemerge, thirsty for redemption.
Strengthen me to walk in the path of bereavement
Upon which my wretched brothers walked,
To knock in vain upon the world's heart
And continue believing in Thee!

— "Harchev Libi, Eli"

In spite of the cruel facts and annihilation, these experiences have not muted the vertiable and genuine voice of faith. It is Jobian truism that vindicated itself fully: "*Hen Yekatleyni Lo Ayachel*" (In spite Thou smitest me, I believe in Thee). *This stubborn faith was never snuffed out in the gas chambers nor eradicated in the tortures sustained by the victims and survivors. With every dying victim another "Shma Israel" emerged from his dying lips. One additional sentence was written in blood into the manifesto of Israel's eternity. With every lash or sadistic beating, the Germanic beast beat into the Jew's consciousness a greater will to live for the day of God's revenge.*

Thus, martyrdom gave birth to its own form of religious ardor, zeal, and faith, unknown hitherto in Jewish history. Our suffering created a novel typology of entreaty and supplication which reflected the mood and attitude of a people while aware of its doom; nevertheless, it provided the authentic spiritual resources upon which the surviving remnant could begin anew to rebuild its shattered life and be an inspiration for a renewed Jewish life and Jewish nationhood.

If faith was ever tested, it never underwent a more crucial test under such tragic circumstances.

If faith is triumphant, then the Jewish people are its witnesses during and after Auschwitz.

NOTES

1. Mark Dworzecky, "Shirah Datit Bagetaot Uvamachanot," (The Religious Poetry of the Ghettos and Concentration Camps), *Shanah B'shanah,* 5721, pp. 304-337.
2. *Ibid.,* p. 309.
3. *Bet-Yaakov,* 21 Iyar, 5721.

VIII

CONCLUSION

And we shall not summon
With distressing cries
Nor will we lacerate ourselves.
We shall not shower our bodies
With flowing tears.
We will only sharpen
Our pain like a knife
And plunge it into the heart
For safe keeping.
And neither God,
Nor Satan,
Not the abyss
Nor the sky
Will ever be able
To erase from our heart
The concealed seal
Which your annihilation
Imprinted upon us.

— Shin Shalom, "Beyteynu He'afel"

We have attempted throughout this study to wrest an authentic expression of the *Shoah* from its poetry. But, to our regret, the horrors of the Holocaust defy human ability to convey the tragic truth. It is beyond expression. Elie Wiesel put it most aptly:

> Auschwitz defies the novelist's language, the historian's analysis, the vision of the prophet. Survivors and witnesses have done their best to describe their experiences, yet their writings have perhaps no substantial relationship with what they have seen and lived through.

Shin Shalom as a poet described this very agonizing truth from his particular poetic perspective in a few telling words:

> And understand,
> And gnash your teeth —
> Amen!
>
> — Ibid

We have seen that there was a profound and compelling awareness among all the people of the Ghettos and Camps to record and convey the terrible truth for the sake of future generations that they might know what befell the Jewish people in full view of the entire world. The most direct and intimate way to accomplish this seemed to be free verse. This is why we have an unusually large quantity of poems which were written with great simplicity, unpretentiously honest, reflecting in many cases limited poetic skill and totally unconscious of any esthetics of language art form. In each of these poems we confront a sacred document of a desperate people, involved as chroniclers of the Holocaust with the urgency to jot down all the details and their emotional reactions to the last chapter of European Jewry.

Not even Yitzchak Katzenelson's epic nor Meir Bossak's great elegy are considered artistically complete works. Their grandeur rests in their writers' historical actuality and authenticity as witnesses and victims.

Thus, the entire gamut of poetry reads like a chronicle of the bloody events perpetrated by the Nazis and their collaborators and the indictment of ethically bankrupt Western Civilization.

Since the poetry was highly individualistic and emotional, it spoke the truth in simple terms free from the embellishments of artistic exploits. It had no time for artistic endeavor. There was not much time left. *Chashticha, Shiri, K'sufah Rechokah* (I sensed you my poem, like a distant storm . . .) Only such verses seem to have retained their shattering impact, they are the most vivid form a written document can ever be. This poetry became a veritable servant of the history of the Holocaust events. For this reason, no Holocaust history will or can be written without resorting to these poetic works. They are permeated with the still living and pulsating emotions of their authors who are no more . . .

We have not found any broad thematic attempt in the Holocaust poetry. The dominant factor is the subjective "I" which reflects from within the entire tragedy: poverty, deprivation, hunger, orphanhood, despair, dehumanization, slavery, torture, flickering hope, wounded faith and confrontation with ultimate death. This unique poetry was in most cases written as an eyewitness account, spontaneous, capturing the horror in all its inhuman barbarity and becoming more intensive and testamental as the end neared.

But again there is an essential difference between the verses written within the annihilation area and the ones written outside.

At the beginning of the Nazi onslaught, not much poetry was written. The poetry that was written was only an echo of a painful outcry. As the events began unfolding in rapid succession, so did poetry keep pace with the tempo of the changing scenes, one more horrendous than its predecessor. Ever since then no authentic Jewish poetry can be written without its roots being deeply grounded in the Holocaust.

Chaim Chamiel, for example, wrote the following poem on the eve of the Twentieth Anniversary of Israel's independence. The joyous occasion was characteristically adumbrated by the sensitive Hebrew poet for whom the burden of the Holocaust memories do not get lighter with the lapse of time. The future Jewish historian will be compelled to reckon with this problem.

I

Pardon me, Lord,
That I do not —
That I cannot
That I cannot yet
Sing of the new miracles
Which were
Drowned
In blood.

II

Forgive me, Lord
That I am still incapable
To praise and write poems:
For my heart
Is still as bitter as an olive
And my words still
Stammer.

III

Pardon me, Lord,
That I do not —
That I cannot
But cry
Over the miracles.
And the cry is
Because of greatness
And of suffering.

IV

Forgive me, Lord,
That I too
Danced with my friends
On the main road
Reaching the hill
But in my head
Still resounded
The songs of the Holocaust.

V

The smile
From my lips
Has melted,
Since then
I avoid laughter
And my heart
Is hollow.

VI

Pardon me, Lord,
That at night
My dream is swallowed
By the knife grinder —
Woe unto me!
My father, my mother
My brothers
And my sisters!

VII

Teach me
How to forgive the decree
Against my people and

How to tear up my vision
And how to love You —
My Father, teach me.

VIII

Pardon me, Lord,
For not being able
As of yet
To sing praises
For the new miracles,
For being yet unable
To compose poems of adoration
For being incapable
Of crying
From greatness
Or from affliction.
That I too
Danced on the highway
Reaching the hill,
For having lost
My smile
And for my dream
That was absorbed
In the knife grinder
Teach me, Lord,
Teach me,
To Love.

— "Slach Li Elohim"

Thus, we have found,that as long as Holocaust poetry remains within the historical and emotional context, it continues to be the voice of Jewish anguish, not as yet able to reconcile itself with the Holocaust tragedy nor able to be comforted, as Yaacov Fichman put it:

May the anger never dissipate
Nor my tears dry up,
And may the Holocaust
Keep buring in my soul
And never be extinguished.

But the moment poetry ventures outside of its emotional orbit and attempts to grasp the meaning of the Holocaust tragedy and conceptualize it, it faces obvious failure.

Before we conclude this study, a word as to the literary placement of the Holocaust poetry is in order. There are three basic categories of literary genre into which the poetry under consideration can be divided: a) lyric, b) epic, and c) pathetic.

A) *Lyrical Poetry*

Within this genre, the authors express their sorrow and pain for the destruction of their world. In the words of Meir Bossak, "Here the light was spread, and here it faded out . . ."

Generally speaking, here poetry succeeded in giving full and cogent expression to the Holocaust event. Because of its personal and intimate nature it concerned itself primarily with personal experiences. On occasion, it departed from its individualism and reflected aspects of the Jewish collective.

B) *Epic Poetry*

There are poets who keenly felt, in a most personal manner, the events that took place. Their empathy dominated their poetic creations. There were also those who themselves were the victims of Holocaust tragedy. Thus the Holocaust ballad came into being from the pens of the victims and empathizers. The dominant theme that repeats itself throughout is the slow agony of a doomed people and the accompanying tragic scenes taking place at the time of departure; on the way to the open pit; at the digging of their own graves; in the description of the exterminated communities; in the memorialization of destroyed synagogues; the cruel death of Rabbis, scholars and disciples; the murder of Rabbinic leaders with their congregations; the tragic death of parents and children, brothers and sisters. The life, agony and murder of simple, wonderful and pious masses of Jews were described here in shattering dramatic terms. Out of this particular poetic genre were created the great epic dramas with a variety of poetic form and skill of serious proportions and scope.[1]

C) *Pathetic Poetry*

Within this genre, pathos and emotionalism reigns supreme. It is full of sorrow and tears. The best example is the last stanza of Shin Shalom's poem, "Galed":

> Six million beheaded heads
> Six million burned bodies
> Six million eyes that spell: atrocity

Six million voices that cry out for help
Six million hearts on fire
The calamity of six million is the testimony . . .

The critic Avraham Hagurni-Green rejects this verbosity and repetitiousness as failing to yield the hoped for results. He suspects that such wordiness leads to too much pathos.[2] Yosef Chanani,[3] on the other hand, maintains that only that sort of poetry which gives expression of its particular times and reflects the generation's spirit, mood and conditions, fights its battles to force self confrontation and makes demands, earns its validity as the generation's spokesman. The poets Israel Efros, Shimon Halkin, Aharon Zeitlin, Chaim Chamiel and Yehuda Leyb Bialer all have admittedly concluded that they were really unable to address themselves to the Holocaust topic as such. All they did was to share their personal sorrow and anguish. They were unable to define the Holocaust from the aspect of its apocalyptic stark and bewildering truth.

Chaim Chamiel contends that there is no accident in the universe. Since he is not God he cannot explain the Holocaust and its horrors. This resembles the question the poet-philosopher Israel Efros posed: "Hashadai Hu O Shed?" (Is he a God or demon), and is certainly not too far from Yehudah Bialer's declaration "It is difficult for me to defend or to accuse the Lord . . ." Bialer bases his statement on the famous answer of the late Chief Rabbi of Israel, Isaac Halevi Herzog, to survivors who asked him where God was during the years of our great suffering . . . He replied in Yiddish: *Ich Vell Nisht Farentfern* (I will not excuse! . . .). In the same vein, Aharon Zeitlin ventures to address with visceral simplicity the most obsessing theological problem that has been occupying the center stage in Jewish thinking: "I cannot live with God in view of the Holocaust, and I cannot live without Him as a Jew; therefore, he declares: *Shiviti Maidanek Lenegdi Tamid, Shiviti Mashiach Lenegdi Tamid!* (I have set forever Maidanek before me, I have set forever the Messiah before me). This excruciating contradiction is the quintessence of our contemporary post-Holocaust thinking.

It is quite obvious, that the poets and the Holocaust historians have not been able to reach any objectivity or perspective on this subject.

In fact, the *Shoah* poetry intrinsically lacks a broad spectrum, for the subject of the Holocaust does not lend itself to too much speculation, if at all. Its veracity is too profound and the facts are too shattering to leave any room for theological or philosophical speculation. Yet the subject compels such an attempt even though its results are most frustrating. The best classical example remains Meir Bossak's poem as a religio-philosophic recitative. In short, the Holocaust-chronicle, whether it was written in prose or verse, was written with the blood of one's heart.

Moreover, the shocking incomprehensibility of the Holocaust seems to have wiped out all the distinct and different theological and philosophical perceptions. They appear to say the same thing although with different emphasis. Thus, the ardent believer in Providence became impatiently daring to raise the ultimate question directly, and seldom defended God's esoteric justice . . . Others who dismissed theodicy altogether often opted to glorify the Jews' relentless will to live and the poeple's unmatched heorism. They preferred to uncover in the ashes of the destruction the living sparks of Israel's future redemption. As to the implacable pessimist, even though he had a ready answer: "There is no judge nor is there any justice," nevertheless, even he refused to despair of the eternity of Israel . . .

As expected, the essential question was not answered nor was any answer even suggested. In this particular aspect we have not found any material difference between the poetry written in the Ghetto and Camps and that which was written outside the Holocaust area. The tone and character of this battle against Heaven depended entriely on the personal views and tempers of the authors. There is no good reason to assume that there was an orchestrated assault of blasphemy against a Silent God. There was a deep-felt bitter outcry of anguish, and since the God of Justice and Compassion has been the only source of our people's hope, He became, consequently, the main target of the people's disappointment. After all, whom could the desperate Jew address, his murderers or his God? At the entrance to the gas-chamber or at the edge of the ravine when the victim stood face to face with his death, what sort of a declaration would one expect to hear of hope or despair, of submission or rebellion? . . .

Yet after all this gruesome and devastating experience, the survivors of Auschwitz and the generation after have been demonstrating undaunted courage to continue, to rebuild, to restore and never despair of redemption. Why? Not simply because of their own merits or the inalienable rights of the future generations, but because of the profound *awareness that a third of the Jewish people died granting the survivors a supreme reason to continue the martyrs' unfinished task.*

Frankly, after Auschwitz, Jewish national continuation can no longer lay its exclusive claim to the pristine covenant between God and Abraham. *After Auschwitz the covenant has been amended with a promise which we made to our martyred people: that it is incumbent upon every Jew now and in the future to be responsible for perpetuating their ideals, hopes, traditions, and faith.*

The attempt by well meaning historians to propose a thesis based on a Hegelian philosophy of history is naive and obviates the central issue: the outright murder of eleven million innocent people, among them a third of the Jewish people, by people who had been raised for generations in Christian ethics and in the values of Western Civilization. This was not a dialectical development of history *per se.* If this were so, we would have to conclude that such a repetition is bound to occur at intervals and its victims would be any people, nation or race chosen at random. We would not, therefore, be entitled to decry it as we do not decry death as a fact of life.

But the fact remains, that the Jewish people were the specific traget of Hitler's program for annihilation, and this success was not accomplished single handedly. His silent partners included the entire Christian world (except for Denmark). For we now know in all the details that the victims of Hilter's "Final Solution" could have been rescued, but such plans were rejected, and persistently refused, for reasons devoid of moral sensitivity and human responsibility.

For this reason Hebrew poetry has reflected primarily the harrowing events and unbearable suffering during the *Shoah* rather than dwelled upon its causes. It reacted with an uncontrolled outcry of indignation and grief. It accused the world of silence and indifference, it condemned its callousness and agonized over its millions of innocent victims. Its verse is permeated with psychological perplexity and an unsettling spiritual trauma, a negative outlook on man, his world, his culture, his ethics, his values and his deceptive civilization. Thus, never before has poetry reflected a deeper sense of despair or a purer sense of faith. Often the incongruous occured: faith lifted from the ashes by the religiously uncommitted; the most blasphemous inveighing against God by the religiously devout; and venomous indictment against man by once-dedicated humanists.

It should, therefore, follow that logically Holocaust poetry —

the testimony in verse *par excellence* — is not subject at any time to pedantic literary criticism. The authors' state of mind and the given conditions prevented the coining of elegant verses with subdued emotions. It is the repository of the cruel facts of the Holocaust written with a raging pen which retains the emotional pain of the author and reveals synoptically the desperate psychological struggle and physical suffering of our people.

To the eternal credit of Jewish poetry in general, and Hebrew poetry in particular, it has gallantly fulfilled its historic task as a recorder of our people's most tragic experience. It has faithfully perpetuated through its verse the terrible truth as it was recorded by its authors regardless of their poetic ability. What is important, is that the poetry served as the most authentic emotional report of the tragic experiences, personal testaments and testimony, and above all the sharing of reactions to the cataclysm as it unfolded. Hence, the poetry that comes from the Holocaust area represents the spirit and facts of an annihilated European Jewry. Because the truth is its most important objective, this poetry often comes to us without embellishments. It comes to tell us what has really occured without verbosity, and its emotionalism betrays the deep despair of people who know that nobody cares. It is, however, as sensitive and shocking as bare truth can be.

On the other hand, the poetry that comes to us from outside the Shoah territory is characteristically reacting most responsively with great emotionalism to the cataclysmic events. It is permeated with empathy and outpouring grief of sick souls and broken hearts. It explodes like a volcano and it pours forth its pain and anguish with burning spontaneity.

Thus, *Shoah* poetry can be epitomized as the poetry of the tortured soul which has its own logic and rationale. It is the unique poetry which attempts to uncover "The Ultimate Secret" of suffering, its anguish and its meaning as verified by some of the living poets themselves.

And finally, in spite of the great merits of poetry's achievement in reflecting all the major themes of the Holocaust, it has not yet attained its fullest grandeur.

Aharon Zeitlin observed that the Holocaust deserves an all embracing great epic which will dwarf the Illiad in its scope and character, befitting the *Shoah* as the greatest tragedy of all times.

Time will eventually create that required perspective. The poetry on hand, with all its literary merits and demerits, will surely serve as the rich treasure house for the future great epic which will give definite expression to the Holocaust.

For the moment, the impressions of this great disaster are still very much alive because of the surviving witnesses in our midst who remind us of the nightmarish horrors, and the outcry of the anguish still reverberates in every thought of ours. In the words of Aharon Zeitlin:

Hashoah Lo Nigmerah V'lo Nigmeret

(The Holocaust has not yet ended and is not a subject that can be concluded.)

— *Beyn Ha'esh V'Hayeshah*

Indeed, we may proclaim with an ardent prayer: "NEVER AGAIN," but the disturbing events in the aftermath of the Holocaust have reflected some very sad facts. Mankind has refused to learn any moral lesson from the Holocaust event. The Holocaust has extended its devastating effects far beyond murder and crematoria. It has evidently deadened human sensitivity and neutralized the little morality that was awakened right after the end of World War II.

What has transpired in the last thirty years full of human degradation, the genocide in Biafra and elsewhere . . . The existence of human suffering and hunger, denial of human rights and human freedom, and the world's continuous silence, needs no elaboration.

The conscious effort to rewrite the Holocaust events while the witnesses are still alive is not done by deranged minds but is symptomatic of the fact that nothing has intrinsically changed. The world wants to forget and forgive with charity the murderers of innocent people and the prisoners of human bestiality.

Almost prophetically, the Hebrew poet Abraham Sholonsky predicted this now prevailing and disappointing attitude of the world, that soon after the massacres, opted rather to forget and forgive rather than care about the implications of the Holocaust for all mankind.

The fires will rise
And reach full devastation . . .
And a day will come
Woe, how shall we welcome it
How shall we face the day of bitter disappointment . . .

Noiseless will it suddenly come
Bring to light the nefarious gallows
Of the extermination places
Which we never could conceive
Nor ever perceive . . .

But the day will surely come . . .

That's the day of oblivion.
It will come hurriedly and
Without anger.
Suddenly and noiselessly will it appear
While somewhere will die
The sound of the last tortured cry . . .

The last cry will die
From upon the mouth and ear . . .
As in days gone by —
The world will be eager to rejoice
Like the Gentile rivers in their moist noise.
As in the days past:
Before Sodom and murder
As if nothing has happened
Even the heart will forget
Instantly forever
Like the forgotten tree in the field.

The sheaves will bend
Before the forgiving winds
Only you my people
Will awake with the morning . . .
Bereaved and inconsolable.

You will awake and no man will be there
All has the wind carried away . . .
Only Jeremiah will still be there
In the barren field alone
Gathering and kissing your remaining bones.

The world that was rescued from demise
Wants to live and covets life . . .
Alas the joyous sounds of tomorrow
Will be painful like a sharp knife

In the flesh of my proud people . . .
Whose remnants will weep
The cry of bitter disappointment . . .

— *Mul Yom Ha'achzavot*

Let us just look at facts. Germany's regained economic might has resulted in the reawakening of German nationalism which invokes the "Statute of Limitations" and aims at freeing summarily all the war criminals who have not as yet been prosecuted. Germany and the rest of the world actually tell us: "Enough of the Nazi story. It's time to forgive and forget!" The Western Hemisphere became the home for many Nazi criminals who are protected by law while East Germany "Kashered" them all by the ritual of Communist Party membership.

Perhaps the introduction of Holocaust studies in High Schools and universities around the world will awaken some people. Perhaps.

For this reason Zeitlin's insight has been invaluable as a scathing commentary of our times: "The Holocaust has not yet ended its story . . ."

As to the great epic the Holocaust deserves, perhaps it may one day be written, but not before man by his own conscious effort has regained his lost divine image and moral posture and redeemed himself from his inhumanity to his fellow man.

NOTES

1. The ballads and the best known dramatic poems are:
   "Harav V'hadayan" by I. Sh. Schwartz
   "Harav Hakavur Ad Tzavar" by Ephraim Lisitzky
   "Misipurey Na'ar Choleh" by David Shimoni
   "Ma'aseh B'asarah Yehudim" by Avraham Broides
   "Reb Mendl Achiv Shel Harabbi Migur" by Shin Shalom
   "Akeydat Rabbi Yirmeyaho" by Yehuda Leib Bialer
2. *L'Nose Hashoah B'shirateynu,* Abraham Hagurni-Green.
3. *Hapoel Hatzair,* Vol. 6, 1951.

Bibliography Of All Authors and Their Works Mentioned In This Study

Akavyahu, Yitzchak. "B'Ma'agley Shirat Shin Shalom," *Karmelit.* Year 6-7.

Alterman, Natan. *Hatur Hashvi'i.* Tel Aviv: Machbarot L'Sifrut, 1962.

Alterman, Natan. *Simchat Ani'im.* Tel Aviv: Machbarot L'Sifrut, 1955.

Amir, Enda (Finkerfeld). "Mima'amakim-Hearot Lapoema Hagedolah L'Meir Bossak," *Hapoel Hatzair.* Year 51, Vol. 29, No. 22. 8 Adar, 1958.

Amir, Enda (Finkerfeld). *Achat.* Tel-Aviv: Dvir, 1960.

Amir, Enda (Finkefeld). *Gadish.* Tel-Aviv: Dvir, 1949.

Amir, Enda (Finkerfeld). "Eim Shakula," *D'var Hashavua.* Vol. 5739. Tel-Aviv: 2 Tammuz, 5704.

Apfelfeld, A.Z. "Shlichut," *Molad.* No. 95. June-July 1956.

Arad, Tzvi, *Nose Hashoah Bashira Haivrit.* Seminar Hakibbutzim, Published 1964.

Arad, Tzvi. *Yoman Ba'efer.* Hakibutz Hameuchad, Merchavia, 1946.

Aran, David. "Hakushiah Hagdolah: Al Leah Goldberg," *Masa,* No. 16. Tel-Aviv: 28 Elul, 1952.

Arkadi, S. *B'chayeyhem Uv'motam.* Tel-Aviv: Am Oved, 1950.

Avineyri, Ari. "Shirah B'terem Shoah," *Masa,* No. 20. Tel-Aviv: Year 26, 1964.

Avinur, Gita. "Mima'amakim, Al Shiro Shel Meir Bossak," *Masa,* No. 16. Tel-Aviv: 28 Nisan, 1958.

Avivi, Shmuel, *Gitzim.* Tel-Aviv: Tarbut, 1956.

Barash, Asher. *Tzel Tzohorayim.* Tel-Aviv: Masada, 1948.

Bartena, Mordechai. *Shirat Ha'eden He'avud.* Jerusalem: Achiasaf, 1947.

Bartini, Kalman. *Marot Al Ha'efer.* Tel-Aviv: D'vir, 1954.

Basok, Moshe. *M'achorey Hazore'a.* Ein Charod, Hakibbutz Hame'uchad, 1949.

Bat Miriam, Yocheved. *Shirim L'Geto.* Merchaviah, Sifriyat Poalim, 1946.

Bavli, Hillel. *Aderet Hashanim.* Jerusalem: Mosad Bialik, 1955.

Ben-Eliezar, Shimon. *"Kneged Hamekonenim," Amudim.* Vol. 33. Tel-Aviv: 1945.

Ben Meir, M. Sh. *Tzel Utzlil. Tel-Aviv: M. Neuman, 1958.*

Ben Menachem, Shabatai. "Bitfutzot Yisrael, Shtikat M'Shorereynu," *Hatzofeh* (Daily), Vol. 3005. 7 Kislev, 1945.

Ben Nachum, Daniel. "Shoat Yisrael Bashirah Haivrit," *Heydim.* Vol. 2. Tel-Aviv: April 1947.

Ben Yosef, Yitzchak. "Kidush Hashem Un'kamah B'Shirat Tschernichovsky," *Hapoel Hatzair.* Vol. 30, No. 38. Year 51.

Bergman, Menachem, *Ben Ha'aretz.* Tel-Aviv: Am Oved, 1947.

Bergman, Sh. H. "Moto Shel Mavet Hearot Al Hapoema Shel Aharon Zeitlin: Bein Haesh V'hayesha," *Hapoel Hatzair.* Vol. 29, No. 27, Year 51, April 1958.

Bergman, Sh. H. "Shalom Lach Eyropa: Hearot Al Shiro Shel Shin Shalom," *Davar* (Daily). Vol. 4904. September 22, 1941.

Berkowitz, Eliezar. *Faith After the Holocaust.* New York: KTAV Publishing House, Inc., 1973.

Berman, Adolf Avraham. "Shirah Min Hat'hom," *Kovetz Yad-Vashem, Mechkarim B'parshyiot Hashoah V'hagvurah*. Jerusalem.
Berman, Nachum. "Ayeka?," *Betzaron*. Year 4. Nisan, 1943.
Bernfeld, Shimon. *Sefer Had'maot*. Berlin: Eshkol, 1924-6.
Bialer, Yehudah Leib. *Ashdot Yamim*. Jerusalem: Mosad Harav Kook, 1957.
Bialik, Ch. N. *Kol Kitvey Ch. N. Bialik*. Tel-Aviv: D'vir, 1951.
Binyamin, H. "Abba Kovner V'Hapoema Ha'ivrit Hamodernit, B'dom Milim Tzlulot-Shirat Hagvurah L'Abba Kovner," *Masa*. No. 11. Tel-Aviv: 17 Tammuz, 1952.
Blaustein, Yitzchak. *Rachamim V'dam. Tel-Aviv: Yabne, 1940.*
Blumenthal, Nachman. "Yitzchak Katzenelson K'historyon Shel T'kufat Hashoah," *Yediot Beit Lochamei Hagetaot*. No. 3. 1954.
Bossak, Meir. *Ve'ata Eynay Ra'atcha*. Tel-Aviv: Galim, 1958.
Broide, Katriel. "Lo Eshkachech Hageto La'ad," see *Prager Anthology*.
Broides, Avraham. *M'aadam L'adam*. Tel-Aviv: Mosad Bialik, 1948.
Broides, Avraham. *Shorashim Basela*. Tel-Aviv: Ayanot, 1956.
Burla, Yehudah. "Al Hapoemot Shel David Shimoni," *Hapoel Hatzayir*. Vol. 24, No. 4. Cheshvan, 1950.
Cahan, Yaakov. *Kol Kitvei Y.C*: Tel-Aviv: D'vir, 1950.
Chamiel, Chaim. *M'ofek El Ofek. Jerusalem: Moreshet, 1952.*
Chelmsky, Ya'akov. "Geto-Riga," *D'var Hapoelet*. No. 1. Sh'vat, 1948.
Chomsky, Dov. *Ey Sham, Shirim*. Jerusalem: Achiasaf, 1945.
Cochrane, Arthur C. "The Church's Confession Under Hilter," *Westminster Conservative Judaism*. Quarterly Organ of the RA Press. Philadelphia, 1962.
Davidon, Ya'akov. *Eytz Hasadeh*. Tel-Aviv: Yabneh, 1954.
Dawidowicz, Lucy S. *The War Against The Jews: 1933-1945*. New York: Holt, Rinehart and Winston, 1975.
Deshe (Eisenstat), Michael. *Urim B'lev Yam*. Tel-Aviv: Yabneh, 1946.
Domnitz, A. "V'acharei He'ason," *Betzaron*. Year 5, Vol. 2. New York City: Cheshvan, 1948.
Donat, Alexander. *The Holocaust Kingdom*. New York: Holt, Rinehart and Winston, 1963.
Dorit, Ida. "Simchat Aniyim L'Natan Alterman," *Masa*. No. 11. Tel-Aviv: 17 Tammuz, 1952.
Dworzetsky, Mark. "Shirah Datit Bagetaot Uvamachanot," *Shana B'hanah*. Erev Rosh Hashanah. 5721/1960.
Efros, Israel. *Anachnu Hador*. New York City: Ogen, 1948.
Egozi, Akiba. Orot Ba'ofel. "Histadrut Ivrit." U.S.A., 1952.
Einstein, Reuben. *The Jewish Spectator*. Pgs. 8-16. June 1967.
Ek, G. ed. "Yediot Yad Vashem." Jerusalem.
Epstein, A. *Shirato Shel Efros, Sefer Hashana L'Yehuday Amerika*. Vol. 7 New York.
Erlich, Israel. *Al Hadam*. Merchavia, Hakibutz Hameuchad, 1946.
Esh, Shaul, ed. *From Hatred to Extermination*. (Seven Essays) Pub. by the Second World Congress of Jewish Studies, August 4, 1957.
Extermination and Resistance, Vol. 1. Israel: Kibbutz Lohamei Hagetaot, 1958.
"The Dignity of the Destroyed," *Judaism*. Summer 1961.

Fackenheim, Emil L. *God's Presence in History.* Harper Torchbooks, 1970.
Fichman, Yaakov. *Pe'at Sadeh.* Jerusalem: Schocken, 1944.
Fichman, Yaakov. *K'tavim.* Tel-Aviv: D'vir, 1950.
Flannery, Edward H. *The Anguish of the Jews.* 4th Edition. London: The MacMillan Co., 1969.
Frankl, Viktor E. *From Death-Camp to Existentialism.* Boston: Beacon Press, 1959.
Frankl, Viktor, E. *Man's Search for Meaning.* 7th Edition. New York City: Washington Square Press, 1965.
Friedlander, Albert. *Out of the Whirlwind.* New York: U.A.H.C., 1968.
Gebirtig, M. "Bi'utei Laylah," see *Prager Anthology.*
Gilad, Zerubavel. *Nigunim Basa'ar.* Ein-Charod, Ḥakibbutz Hameuachad, 1946.
Gilboa, Amir. *Shirim Baboker Baboker.* Merchavia Hakibutz Hameuchad, 1953.
Glatstein, Jacob, I. Knox, S. Margoshes, eds. *Anthology of Holocaust Literature.* Philadelphia: JPS, 1969.
Glazar, Rilka. "Karon Mavet," see *Prager Anthology.*
Glickson, Moshe. *The Jewish Comples of Karl Marx.* Pamphlet No. 20. New York City: Herzl Press, 1961.
Goldberg, Leah. *Al Hapricha.* Sifriat Poalim, Merchavia, 1948.
Gordon, Jacques. "Ha'od Nisharu Lanu Yamim Harbe?", see *Prager Anthology.*
Greenberg, Uri Tzvi. *R'chovot Hanahar.* Jerusalem: Schocken, 1951.
Grinboim, Yitzchak, ed. *Encyclopedia Shel Galuyot.* Tel-Aviv: 1953.
Guri, Chaim. *Pirchei Esh.* Merchavia, Sifriat Poalim, 1948.
Gutman, Yisrael. *Anashim Va'efer.* Merchavia, Sifriat Poalim, 1957.
Gutman, Yisrael and Livia Rothkirchen, eds. *The Catastrophe of European Jewry.* Jerusalem: Yad Vashem, 1976.
Haberman, A. M., ed. *Sefer Gzeirot Ashkenaz Vetzarfat.* Jerusalem: Tarshish, 1946.
Haesler, Alfred A. *The Lifeboat Is Full.* New York: Funk & Wagnalls, 1969.
Hagorni-Green, A. *L'Nose Hashoah B'shirateynu.* Tel-Aviv: Eked, 1970.
Halevi, Zerach. "Rachell Mevakah Al Baneha," *Emunim.* Pinchas Peli, ed. Jerusalem: Mosad Bialik.
Halkin, Shimon. *Al Ha'i.* Jerusalem: Mosad Bialik, 1946.
Halkin, Shimon, *Modern Hebrew Literature.* New Edition. New York: Schocken Books, 1970.
Halperin, Irving. "Hitnagdut Haruchanit B'sifrut Hashoah," *Kovetz Yad-Vashem.* No. 7. Jerusalem.
Hameiri, Avigdor, *Hamoked Haran.* Tel-Aviv: Mosad Bialik, D'vir, 1944.
Hausner, Gideon. *Justice in Jerusalem.* New York: Schocken Books, 1968.
Hilberg, Raul. *Documents of Destruction.* Chicago: Quadrangle Press, 1971.
Hilberg, Raul. *The Destruction of the European Jews.* Chicago: Quadrangle Books. 1961.
Holtz, Avraham. "Al Chet," First time appeared in *Conservative Judaism* (Quarterly). The entire "Al Chet" is integrated in the new H.H.D. Conservative Prayer Book published by Rabbinical Assembly of America.
Huberband, Shimon. *Kidush Hashem.* Jerusalem: Zachor, 1969.
Indelman, Elchanan. *Even Li Ekach.* Jerusalem: Kiryat Sefer, 1957.
Ivri, Yitzchak. *Ben Dam L'Dam.* Tel-Aviv: Yabneh, 1940.
Journal of Ecumenical Studies. Philadelphia, Pa: Temple Univ.

Judaism (Quarterly). Published by American Jewish Committee. Prof. Robert Gordis, ed.
Kariv, Avraham. "Hayehudi Hanizchi El Eretz Amalek." *Davar,* Yearbook 1952.
Karni, Yehudah. *Shir Vadema.* Tel-Aviv: Machbarot L'Sifrut, 1948.
Katzenelson, Gideon. M'Gilat Haesh Shel Dor Hashoah, *Mozhayim.* Vol. 11. 1960.
Katzenelson, Yitzchak. "Hashir al Ha'am Hayehudi Sheneherag," *Ketavim Acharonim.* Beyt Lochamey Hagetaot, 1960.
Kirshenboim, Sh. L. *Toldot Am Israel B'Doreynu.* Tel-Aviv: Amanut, 1955.
Kovner, Abba. *Achoti Hak'tana.* Sifriat Poalim, Merchavia, 1957.
Kurtzvayl, Baruch. "Chazon Ha'ovdan V'hageulah B'shirei Uri Tzvi Greenberg," *Haaretz* (Daily). Vol. 9238.
Lamdan, Yitzchak. *B'ma'alah Akrabim.* Jerusalem: Mosad Bialik, 1948.
Landoi, Yehoshua. "Azaka," *Kol Yisrael.* Year 21, Vol. 21. 1942.
Langer, Lawrence L. *The Holocaust and the Literary Imagination.* Yale University Press, 1973.
Leif, Chaim. "Shirato Shel Yitzchak Lamdan," *Hadoar.* Year 39, Vol. 32. New York: Tamuz, 1950.
Leivick, H. "Mu'amad L'treblinki," *Mivchar Shirat Yiddish.* Hakibutz Hameuchad, ed. Moshe Basok, 1963.
Levi-Linser, H. *Ani Ma'amin.* Tel-Aviv: Orah, 1966.
Levin, Nora. *The Holocaust.* New York: Thamos Y. Crowell Co., 1968.
Lichtenboim, A. "Hameytim," *Hapoel Hatzair.* No. 21. Tel-Aviv: Adar, 1948.
Lisitzky, Ephraim. *Nehogot M'arafel. Tel-Aviv: Ogen-Masada, 1957.*
Lisitzky, Ephraim. *Biymey Shoah Umashu'a.* New York: Ogen, 1960.
Littell, Franklin H. *The Crucifixion of the Jews.* New York: Harper & Row, 1975.
Luria, Yerucham. "Uvikranot Meytim," (see below Mordecai, B.).
Mab'shan, M. *M'oznaim.* Vol. 3-4. Iyar-Sivan 5704.
Maitus, Eliyahu. "Hamilchama V'hashira Haivri't, *Mishmar.* Jerusalem: October 3, 1944.
Margalit, A. "Shisha Million," *Bet Ya'akov.* Year 2, Vol. XI. 1961.
Mark, Ber. *Uprising in the Warsaw Ghetto.* New York: Schocken Books, 1975.
Marx, Karl. *A World Without Jews.* New York: The Wisdom Library, 1959.
Meltzar, Shimshon. *Sefer Hashirot V'habaladot.* Tel-Aviv: Davar, 1951.
Michali, Binyamin Yitzchak. "Hamilchama V'shoat Yisrael B'shirateynu," *Divrei Sofrim.* 1944.
Mordechai, B. and Y. Chanani, eds. *Even M'kir Tizak.* Tel-Aviv: 1945.
Mohar, Meir. *Ayin B'ayin.* Tel-Aviv: D'vir, 1950.
Morse, Arthur D. *While Six Million Died.* New York: Random House, Inc., 1967.
Negev, Rachel. "Yizkor," *M'oznayim.* Year 1, Vol. XI. Adar II, 1940.
Neher, Andre. *Speech and Silence in Prophecy.* El Ha'ayin No.4. Dept. for Ed. and Culture in the Diaspora, WZO and the World Jewish Bible Society. Jerusalem, 1969.
Nesher, Tzvi. "Shirim Mikıryat Mavet," *Mibafnim.* Sivan, 1954.
Neshkes, Shachna. "Kir'u Shamayim," *Mibafnim,* Iyar, 1942.
Ogen, Yitzchak. *B'za'af Haleyl.* Jerusalem: Reuven Mass, 1943.
Ogen, Yitzchak. *Al Gesher Haleil.* Tel-Aviv: N. Tversky, 1947.
Patai, Yosef. "Eichah Shafalta Adam," *Haolam.* Year 34, Vol. 9. 1945.

Peli, Pinchas. "Lama Azavtichem," *Emunim*. Jerusalem: Mosad Harav Kook, 1956.
Peli, Pinchas. "Al Hadam," *Hapoel Hatzayir*. No. 46. August 12, 1947.
Pilch, Judah, ed. *The Jewish Catastrophe in Europe*. New York: The American Association for Jewish Education, 1968.
Pilch, Yehudah. "Al Shir Echad L'Efros: Zunu Za'apeynu," *Hadoar*. Year 42, Vol. 30. New York: 22 Sivan, 1963.
P'niel (Plantovsky), Noaeh. *Al Pitchey T'hom*. Jerusalem: Kiryat Sefer, 1947.
Poliakov, Leon. *Harvest of Hate*. Philadelphia: JPS, 1954.
Prager, Moshe, *Min Hameytzar Karati*. (*Prager Anthology*) Jerusalem: Mosad Harave Kook, 1955.
Rabinowitz, Yasha. "Tzava'a," see *Prager Anthology*.
Ravkay, Yisrael. "Shcharchoret Adumah," *Al Hamishmar*. Vol. 1632. October 12, 1948.
Ravkay, Yisrael. "Al Shirat Hashoah," *Itim*. Year 2, Vol. 20-22. March 3, 1948.
Raz, Shaul. "Tiferer Yichudeynu," *Emunim*. Jerusalem: Mosad Harav Kook, 1956.
Reitlinger, Gerald. *The Final Solution*. New York: The Beechhurst Press, 1953.
Rimon, Yaakov, "Ani Bocheh Al Churban Haolam," *Sne*. Tel Aviv: 1946.
Ringelblum, Emanuel. *Notes From the Warsaw Ghetto*. New York: Schocken Books, 1974.
Robinson, Jacob. *And the Crooked Shall Be Made Straight*. Philadelphia: JPS, 1965.
Robinson, Jacob and Philip Friedman. *Guide to Jewish History Under Nazi Impact*. Yivo Publication.
Rosenblum, Noach. "Hateguvot L'Hastarat Panim B'shirat Hashoah," *Sura*. Vol. 4. New York: 1964.
Rotman, Baruch. "Na'alayim," *Haolam*. Vol. 26-27. Nisan, 1948.
Rubenstein, Richard L. *After Auschwitz*. Indianapolis, The Bobbs-Merril Co., 1966.
Rudin, Elisha. "Laben," *Antologia MiBialik Ad Yameynu*. Tel-Aviv: NIV, 1953.
Schwartz, A. Sh. *Shirim*. Jerusalem: M. Neuman, 1959.
Seh-Lavan, Yosef. "K'ev V'emunah B'shirat Shimonovitch," *L'achdut Ha'avodah* Vol. 29. January 19. 1945.
Sendo, David. *Or Haleylot*. Merchavia, Sifriyat Poalim, 1949.
Shalev, Yitzchak. *Kol Enut*. Jerusalem: Kiryat Sefer, 1955.
Shalom, Shin. *Olam B'lahavot*. Tel-Aviv: Yabneh, 1940.
Shalom, Shin. *Panim El Panim*. Tel-Aviv: Mosad Bialik, 1941.
Shalom, Shin. *Shirim*. Tel-Aviv: Yabneh, 1949.
Shalom, Shin. *Yilan Bachut*. Tel-Aviv: Yabneh, 1946.
Shenker, Sh. "Halev Nilchatz," see *Prager Anthology*.
Shimoni, David. *Shirim*. Vol. I & II. Tel-Aviv: Masada, 1949.
Shirer, William L. *The Rise and Fall of the Third Reich*. Greenville, Conn.: Crest Book, 1962.
Shlonsky, Avraham. *Shirim*. Vol. II. Merchavia, Sifriyat Poalim, 1954.
Shlonsky, Avraham. *K'tavim*. Tel-Aviv: Sifriyat Poalim, 1972.
Shmueli, Efraim. "Grafomania Tragit?" *Al Hamishmar*. December 24, 1948.
Shneur, Zalman. *Kol Kitvei*. Z. Sh. Tel-Aviv: D'vir, 1960.
Shneur Zalman. *Shirim*. Vol. I. Tel-Aviv: Am Oved, 1956.
Shneurson, Fishl. *Psychologia Shel Shoah Ut'kumah*. Tel-Aviv: Yizrael, 1968.
Shtein, Sh. *Shivrei Haleluyah. Tel-Aviv: N'hogot, 1961.*

Skelsky, Yitzchak. "Hazyd Haacharon," *Cherut Annaul.* 1954.
Sutzkever, Avraham. *Charut Aley Luach.* Merchavia, Sifriyat Poalim, 1949.
Tabenkin, Moshe. *Shirim.* Ein Charod; Hakibutz Hameuchad, 1954.
Tanay, Shlomo. "Reyach Ha'esh," *Moznayim.* Tel-Aviv: Sivan, 1945.
Temkin, Mordechai. *B'elem Shir.* Jerusalem: Mosad Bialik, 1956.
Tenenboim (Tene), Binyamin. *B'cheret D'vay.* Merchavia, Sifriyat Poalim, 1945.
The Black Book of Polish Jewry. New York: Roy Publishing, 1943.
Trunk, Isaiah. *Judenrat.* New York: The MacMillan Co., 1972.
Tschernichovsky, Shaul. *Shirim.* Tel-Aviv: Schocken Books, 1953.
Unger, Eliezer. *Zachor.* Tel-Aviv: Masadah, 1945.
Vayntroyb, R. *Gachaley Esh.* Tel-Aviv: Alef, 1967.
Vered, Chaya. *Shirim Al Cherev Umeytar.* Tel-Aviv: Hakibutz Hameuchad, 1955.
Volfovsky, M.Z. *Shirim Upoemot.* Tel-Aviv: Hakibut Hameuchad, 1953.
Weinryb, Bernard. D. *The Jews of Poland.* Philadelphia: JPS, 1973.
Weissmandle, Michel Dov. "Shma Yisroel," *Bet Ya'akov.* 21 Iyar, 5721.
Wiesel, Elie. *Night.* New York City: Avon, Discus Edition, 1969.
Wiesel, Elie. *The Gates of the Forest.* New York City: An Avon Library Book, 1969.
Wiesel, Elie. *Dawn.* New York City: Avon Books, 1970.
Wiesel, Elie. *The Accident.* New York City: Avon, Bard Books, 1970.
Wiesel, Elie. *The Town Beyond the Wall.* New York City: An Avon Library Book, 1969.
Wyschograd, Michael. "Faith and the Holocaust," *Judaism.* Summer 1971.
Yoskovitz, A.A. *P'rachim Nugim.* Tel-Aviv: Yedidim, 1949.
Zachin, Dov. "Sofreinu L'nochach Hashoah," *Mishmar.* Vol. 204. 14 Nisan, 1944.
Zahn, Gordon C. *German Catholics and Hitler's War.* New York City: Sheed & Ward, Inc., 1962.
Zaretzki, Eliyahu. "Geto Lachva," *Hadoar.* Vol. 14. Sivan, 1949.
Zeitlin, Aharon. *Beyn Ha'aesh V'hayesha.* Tel-Aviv: Yabneh, 1957.
Zeitlin, Aharon. "Sod Hamedinah B'sod Maidanek Shaluv," *Hadoar.* Vol. 28. Iyar, 1951.
Zeitlin, Aharon. "Davar Al Yitzchak Katzenelson," *Mibafnim.* Vol. 28, No. 4. Cheshvan, November 1963.
Zeitlin, Aharon. *Shirim Upoemot.* Jerusalem: Mosad Bialik, 1950.
Zimorah, Yisrael. "Al Sifrut Hashoah," *Machbarot L'Sifrut.* March 1953.
Zimorah, Yisrael. "Rechovot Hanahar Shel Uri Zvi Greenberg," *Machbarot L'Sifrut,* No. 5. 1952.
Zisenwine, David W., ed. *Anti-Semitism in Europe: Sources of the Holocaust.* New York: Behrman House, 1976.